Berkeley Protocol

on Digital Open Source Investigations

A Practical Guide on the Effective Use of Digital Open Source
Information in Investigating Violations of International Criminal,
Human Rights and Humanitarian Law

HUMAN
RIGHTS
CENTER

UC Berkeley School of Law

UNITED NATIONS
HUMAN RIGHTS
OFFICE OF THE HIGH COMMISSIONER

New York and Geneva, 2022

This work is co-published by the United Nations, on behalf of the Office of the United Nations High Commissioner for Human Rights (OHCHR), and the Human Rights Center at the University of California, Berkeley, School of Law.

Requests to reproduce excerpts or to photocopy should be addressed to the Copyright Clearance Center at copyright.com.

All other queries on rights and licences, including subsidiary rights, should be addressed to: United Nations Publications, 405 East 42nd Street, S-09FW001, New York, NY 10017, United States of America. Email: Permissions@un.org; website: Shop.un.org.

The designations employed and the presentation of the material in this publication do not imply the expression of any opinion whatsoever on the part of the Secretariat of the United Nations concerning the legal status of any country, territory, city or area, or of its authorities, or concerning the delimitation of its frontiers or boundaries.

Symbols of United Nations documents are composed of capital letters combined with figures. Mention of such a figure indicates a reference to a United Nations document.

Cover image credit: deepfake satellite image created by Ahmed Elgamal using the artificial intelligence platform Playform.

The Human Rights Center at the University of California, Berkeley, School of Law gratefully acknowledges the financial support received from the following donors: the Sigrid Rausing Trust; the Oak Foundation; individual donors at the University of California, Berkeley; Open Society Foundations; and the Rockefeller Foundation Bellagio Center.

Contents

Foreword

Since the early 1990s, digital tools and the Internet, like the camera and telephone before them, have revolutionized how we obtain, collect and disseminate information about human rights violations and other serious breaches of international law, including international crimes.

Today, investigators can capture data about potential human rights violations and other serious breaches of international law, including international crimes, from a vast array of publicly available satellite imagery, videos and photographs, including material uploaded to the Internet from smartphones and posts to social media platforms. This development has helped investigators to bypass government and other traditional information gatekeepers to access key information regarding wrongdoing, even in real time, that would otherwise remain hidden from public view.

Digital open source information has, however, been used in a largely ad hoc manner as human rights organizations, intergovernmental bodies, investigative mechanisms and courts have at times struggled to adapt their working practices to include new digital methods of fact-finding and analysis. One of the greatest challenges that they face is dealing with the discovery and verification of relevant material within an increasing volume of online information, especially photographs and videos captured on smartphones and other mobile devices, some of which may be compromised or misattributed.

Meanwhile, the emergence of international criminal courts and investigative mechanisms, as well as national war crimes units, has further heightened the need for common standards for capturing, preserving and analysing open source information that can be introduced as evidence in criminal trials. For open source information to be admissible as evidence in court, prosecutors and counsel must typically be able to establish its authenticity and chain of custody. Appropriate handling and processing of this material will greatly increase the likelihood that it can be used by prosecutors and counsel. If, however, unsound methods of collection and preservation are used, the information cannot be regarded as reliable for the purposes of establishing facts in a case. Courts and investigative mechanisms will benefit from clear criteria for assessing the weight of open source information either as linkage or crime-based evidence. Common methodological standards on authentication and verification will equally serve human rights fact-finding missions, which also increasingly incorporate digital open source materials in their investigations. Commissions of inquiry, human rights components of peacekeeping operations, field offices of the Office of the United Nations High Commissioner for Human Rights (OHCHR) and other United Nations human rights monitoring and investigation efforts all stand to benefit from sound methodological principles and approaches to support the validity and weight of their findings.

To address this need, our institutions, the Human Rights Center at the University of California, Berkeley, School of Law and OHCHR, have joined forces to publish the *Berkeley Protocol on Digital Open Source Investigations: A Practical Guide on the Effective Use of Digital Open Source Information in Investigating Violations of International Criminal, Human Rights and Humanitarian Law*. The path leading to this publication began on the Berkeley campus in 2009, when the Human Rights Center brought together legal experts, technologists, journalists and activists to develop strategies for using digital technologies and methodologies to expose and document human rights violations. Since then, the Human Rights Center has convened a series of interdisciplinary workshops, in collaboration with a range of technical, legal and methodological experts, including from OHCHR, to brainstorm, to develop new tools and to identify and distil criteria, standards and methods for uncovering, assessing, verifying and preserving digital open source information to document human rights abuses and bring perpetrators to justice. This process aligned well with the efforts of OHCHR to develop guidance and tools to support and advise United Nations commissions of inquiry and fact-finding missions and OHCHR staff in their increasing use of open source information in fact-finding and investigative work.

The development of the Berkeley Protocol benefited from the contributions of individuals with diverse professional perspectives, legal and cultural backgrounds, genders and nationalities and involved more than 150 consultations with experts and input from key stakeholders, including United Nations human rights investigators. It also drew upon the expertise of specialized working groups from the Methodology, Education and Training Section of OHCHR and the Office of the Prosecutor of the International Criminal Court. In accordance with international standards on the development of new methodology, OHCHR and the Human Rights Center subjected the Berkeley Protocol to a rigorous process of review, revision and validation.

Building on this collaborative approach, the Berkeley Protocol includes international standards for conducting online research into alleged violations of international human rights law and international humanitarian and criminal law. It also provides guidance on methodologies and procedures for gathering, analysing and preserving digital information in a professional, legal and ethical manner. Lastly, the Berkeley Protocol sets out measures that online investigators can take to protect the digital, physical and psychosocial safety of themselves and others, including witnesses, victims and first responders (e.g. citizens, activists and journalists), who risk their own well-being to document human rights violations and serious breaches of international law.

The Berkeley Protocol follows in the footsteps of two earlier United Nations protocols: the Minnesota Protocol on the Investigation of Potentially Unlawful Death (1991, updated in 2016), and the Manual on the Effective Investigation and Documentation of

Torture and Other Cruel, Inhuman or Degrading Treatment or Punishment (Istanbul Protocol) (1999, updated in 2004). The Minnesota Protocol, developed by lawyers and forensic scientists engaged in the search for disappeared persons in the 1980s, establishes international standards and procedures for conducting medico-legal investigations into suspicious or unattended deaths, and serves as a means for evaluating the credibility of such investigations. Similarly, the Istanbul Protocol provides guidance to medical practitioners and lawyers on how to recognize and document the physical and psychosocial sequelae of torture so that documentation may serve as valid evidence in court or in other contexts, including human rights investigations and monitoring. All three protocols are founded on the belief that science, technology and law can – and must – work together at the service of human rights. Like the previous protocols, the Berkeley Protocol will be made available in the official languages of the United Nations in order to facilitate its use and utility worldwide.

It is our hope that, in an increasingly digitalized world, the Berkeley Protocol will help online investigators – be they legal professionals, human rights defenders, journalists or others – to develop and implement effective procedures for documenting and verifying violations of international human rights law and international humanitarian and criminal law, making the best use of digital open source information, so that those who are responsible for such violations can be fairly brought to justice.

Eric Stover
Faculty Director, Human Rights Center,
University of California, Berkeley, School of Law

Michelle Bachelet
United Nations
High Commissioner for Human Rights

Executive summary

Open source investigations are investigations that rely, in whole or in part, on publicly available information to conduct formal and systematic online inquiries into alleged wrongdoing. Today, large quantities of publicly available information are accessible through the Internet, where a quickly evolving digital landscape has led to new types and sources of information that could assist in the investigation of alleged human rights violations and serious international crimes. The ability to investigate such allegations is of particular value to investigators who cannot physically access crime scenes in a timely manner, which is often the case in international investigations.

Open source information can provide leads, support intelligence outputs and serve as direct evidence in courts of law. However, in order for it to be used in formal investigation processes, including legal investigations, fact-finding missions and commissions of inquiry, investigators must employ consistent methods, which both strengthen the accuracy of their findings and allow judges and other fact-finders to better evaluate the quality of the investigation process itself. The Berkeley Protocol on Digital Open Source Investigations was developed to provide international standards and guidance for investigators in the fields of international criminal justice and human rights. Such investigators come from a range of institutions, including media outlets, civil society groups and non-governmental organizations, international organizations, courts, and national and international investigative agencies. The establishment of consistent and measurable standards to support this multidisciplinary arena is a means of professionalizing the practice of open source investigations.

While guidelines and training on the use of specific tools and software are an essential part of improving the quality of digital open source investigations, the Berkeley Protocol does not focus on specific technologies, platforms, software or tools, but rather on the underlying principles and methodologies that can be consistently applied, even as the technology itself changes. These principles outline minimum legal and ethical standards for conducting effective open source investigations. By following the guidance in the Berkeley Protocol, investigators will help to ensure the quality of their work, while minimizing the physical, psychosocial and digital risks to themselves and others.

The Berkeley Protocol is designed as a teaching tool and a reference guide for open source investigators. Following an introductory chapter, the subsequent three chapters are dedicated to overarching frameworks, including principles, legal considerations and security. The remaining chapters are focused on the investigation process itself. This section of the Berkeley Protocol begins with a chapter on preparation and strategic planning, followed by a chapter dedicated to the various investigatory steps required – namely, online inquiries, preliminary assessment, collection, preservation, verification and investigative analysis. It concludes with a chapter on the methodology and principles for reporting on the findings of an open source investigation.

Contributors and participants

Berkeley Protocol Coordinating Committee

Lindsay Freeman, Senior Legal Researcher, Human Rights Center, University of California, Berkeley, School of Law

Alexa Koenig, Executive Director, Human Rights Center, University of California, Berkeley, School of Law

Eric Stover, Faculty Director, Human Rights Center, University of California, Berkeley, School of Law

Berkeley Protocol Editorial Committee

Sareta Ashraph, Senior Legal Consultant; Barrister, Garden Court Chambers; former Senior Analyst, United Nations Investigative Team to Promote Accountability for Crimes Committed by Da'esh/Islamic State in Iraq and the Levant

Alix Dunn, Executive Director, The Engine Room

Richard Goldstone, former Justice, Constitutional Court of South Africa; former Chief Prosecutor, International Tribunal for the Former Yugoslavia and the International Criminal Tribunal for Rwanda

Brenda J. Hollis, International Co-Prosecutor, Extraordinary Chambers in the Courts of Cambodia; former Chief Prosecutor, Residual Special Court for Sierra Leone

Tanya Karanasios, Director of Programmes, WITNESS

Enrique Piracés, Media and Human Rights Programme Manager, Center for Human Rights Science, Carnegie Mellon University

Beth Van Schaack, Visiting Professor in Human Rights, Stanford Law School; former Deputy to the Ambassador-at-Large for War Crimes Issues, Office of Global Criminal Justice, United States Department of State

Michel de Smedt, Director, Investigations Division, Office of the Prosecutor, International Criminal Court

Alan Tieger, Senior Trial Attorney, Kosovo Specialist Prosecutor's Office; former Senior Trial Lawyer, International Tribunal for the Former Yugoslavia

Christian Wenaweser, Permanent Representative of Liechtenstein to the United Nations; former President, Assembly of States Parties to the Rome Statute of the International Criminal Court

Alex Whiting, Head of Investigations, Kosovo Specialist Prosecutor's Office; Professor of Practice, Harvard Law School; former Prosecutions Coordinator and Investigations Coordinator, Office of the Prosecutor, International Criminal Court

Susan Wolfinbarger, Foreign Affairs Officer and Analytics Team Lead, United States Department of State; former Senior Project Director, Geospatial Technologies Project, American Association for the Advancement of Science

Berkeley Protocol Advisory Committee

Federica D'Alessandra, Executive Director, Oxford Programme on International Peace and Security, University of Oxford; editor of the Public International Law and Policy Group's *Handbook on Civil Society Documentation of Serious Human Rights Violations: Principles & Best Practices*

Stuart Casey-Maslen, Honorary Professor, Faculty of Law, University of Pretoria; contributor to the *Minnesota Protocol on the Investigation of Potentially Unlawful Death* (2016)

Alison Cole, Specialist Adviser on Human Rights, Department of Internal Affairs, New Zealand

Francoise Hampson, Emeritus Professor,University of Essex School of Law; member of the Commission of Inquiry on Burundi

Christof Heyns, Professor of Human Rights Law, University of Pretoria; member of the Human Rights Committee; former Special Rapporteur on extrajudicial, summary or arbitrary executions; coordinator of the *Minnesota Protocol on the Investigation of Potentially Unlawful Death* (2016)

Vincent Iacopino, Senior Medical Adviser, Physicians for Human Rights; main contributor to the *Manual on the Effective Investigation and Documentation of Torture and Other Cruel, Inhuman or Degrading Treatment or Punishment* (Istanbul Protocol)

Kelly Matheson, Senior Attorney and Programme Manager, WITNESS; author of *Video as Evidence Field Guide*

Hanny Megally, Commissioner, Independent International Commission of Inquiry on the Syrian Arab Republic; Senior Fellow, Center on International Cooperation, New York University

Juan Méndez, Professor of Human Rights Law in Residence, Washington College of Law; former Special Rapporteur on torture and other cruel, inhuman or degrading treatment or punishment; coordinator of the universal protocol for investigative interviewing and procedural safeguards

Aryeh Neier, President Emeritus, Open Society Foundations

Navi Pillay, President, International Commission against the Death Penalty; former United Nations High Commissioner for Human Rights; former judge, International Criminal Court; former President, International Criminal Tribunal for Rwanda

Paulo Sérgio Pinheiro, Chair, Independent International Commission of Inquiry on the Syrian Arab Republic; former Special Rapporteur on the situation of human rights in Burundi; former Special Rapporteur on the situation of human rights in Myanmar

Thomas Probert, Extraordinary Lecturer, Centre for Human Rights, University of Pretoria; Research Associate, Centre of Governance and Human Rights, University of Cambridge; contributor to the *Minnesota Protocol on the Investigation of Potentially Unlawful Death* (2016)

Stephen Rapp, Distinguished Fellow, Simon-Skjodt Center for the Prevention of Genocide, United States Holocaust Memorial Museum; former Ambassador-at-Large for War Crimes Issues, Office of Global Criminal Justice, United States Department of State; former Prosecutor, Special Court for Sierra Leone

Cristina Ribeiro, Investigations Coordinator, Office of the Prosecutor, International Criminal Court

Patricia Sellers, Special Adviser on Gender to the Prosecutor of the International Criminal Court; Visiting Fellow, Kellogg College, University of Oxford; former Legal Adviser and Trial Attorney, International Tribunal for the Former Yugoslavia and International Criminal Tribunal for Rwanda

Workshop participants

Workshop on the New Forensics: Using Open Source Information to Investigate Grave Crimes (Bellagio, Italy, 2017)

Hadi Al Khatib, Syrian Archive

Stuart Casey-Maslen, University of Pretoria

Yvan Cuypers, International Criminal Court

Scott Edwards, Amnesty International

Lindsay Freeman, Human Rights Center, University of California, Berkeley, School of Law

Alexa Koenig, Human Rights Center, University of California, Berkeley, School of Law

Steve Kostas, Open Society Justice Initiative

Andrea Lampros, Human Rights Center, University of California, Berkeley, School of Law

Kelly Matheson, WITNESS

Félim McMahon, International Criminal Court

Julian Nicholls, International Criminal Court

Thomas Probert, University of Cambridge

Cristina Ribeiro, International Criminal Court

Gavin Sheridan, Vizlegal

Eric Stover, Human Rights Center, University of California, Berkeley, School of Law

Alan Tieger, International Tribunal for the Former Yugoslavia

Mark Watson, Commission for International Justice and Accountability

Guy Willoughby, Association for the Study of War Crimes

Workshop on Building an Ethical Framework for Open Source Investigations (University of Essex, United Kingdom, 2019)

Fred Abrahams, Human Rights Watch

Leenah Bassouni, Human Rights Center, University of California, Berkeley, School of Law

Federica D'Alessandra, University of Oxford

Sam Dubberley, Amnesty International

Jennifer Easterday, JustPeace Labs

Scott Edwards, Amnesty International

Lindsay Freeman, Human Rights Center, University of California, Berkeley, School of Law

Geoff Gilbert, University of Essex

Christopher "Kip" Hale, Commission for International Justice and Accountability

Evanna Hu, Omelas

Gabriela Ivens, Mozilla Fellow and WITNESS

Alexa Koenig, Human Rights Center, University of California, Berkeley, School of Law

Matt Mahmoudi, University of Cambridge

Lorna McGregor, University of Essex

Daragh Murray, University of Essex

Vivian Ng, University of Essex

Enrique Piracés, Center for Human Rights Science, Carnegie Mellon University

Zara Rahman, The Engine Room

Sasha Robehmed, The Engine Room

Ilia Siatitsa, Privacy International

OHCHR representative, from the Methodology, Education and Training Section

Round Table on Legal Issues Arising from Open Source Investigations (The Hague, 2019)

David Akerson, United Nations Investigative Team to Promote Accountability for Crimes Committed by Da'esh/Islamic State in Iraq and the Levant

Sareta Ashraph, Garden Court Chambers

Danya Chaikel, Kosovo Specialist Prosecutor's Office

Alan Clark, International Criminal Court

Federica D'Alessandra, University of Oxford

Nico Dekens, Bellingcat

Chris Engels, Commission for International Justice and Accountability

Lindsay Freeman, Human Rights Center, University of California, Berkeley, School of Law

Emma Irving, Leiden University

Michelle Jarvis, International, Impartial and Independent Mechanism to Assist in the Investigation and Prosecution of Persons Responsible for the Most Serious Crimes under International Law Committed in the Syrian Arab Republic since March 2011

Edward Jeremy, International Criminal Court

Ashley Jordana, Global Rights Compliance

Sang-Min Kim, Human Rights Center, University of California, Berkeley, School of Law

Alexa Koenig, Human Rights Center, University of California, Berkeley, School of Law

Nicholas Koumjian, Independent Investigative Mechanism for Myanmar

Bastiaan Van Der Laaken, International, Impartial and Independent Mechanism to Assist in the Investigation and Prosecution of Persons Responsible for the Most Serious Crimes under International Law Committed in the Syrian Arab Republic since March 2011

Dearbhla Minogue, Global Legal Action Network

Nick Ortiz, Leiden University

Matevz Pezdirc, Genocide Network of the European Union Agency for Criminal Justice Cooperation

Sanja Popovic, Kosovo Specialist Prosecutor's Office

Steven Powles, Doughty Street Chambers; International Bar Association's War Crimes Committee

Stephen Rapp, Simon-Skjodt Center for the Prevention of Genocide, United States Holocaust Memorial Museum

Cristina Ribeiro, International Criminal Court

Mark Robson, Commission for International Justice and Accountability

Brad Samuels, SITU Research

Dalila Seoane, Civitas Maxima

Carsten Stahn, Leiden University

Melinda Taylor, International Criminal Court

Alan Tieger, Kosovo Specialist Prosecutor's Office

Raquel Vázquez Llorente, eyeWitness to Atrocities

Additional expert reviewers

Elise Baker, Human Rights Center, University of California, Berkeley, School of Law

Sean Brooks, Center for Long-Term Cybersecurity, University of California, Berkeley

Stephanie Croft, Human Rights Center, University of California, Berkeley, School of Law

Sam Dubberley, Amnesty International

Thomas Edwin, Center for Advanced Defense Studies

Christopher "Kip" Hale, Commission for International Justice and Accountability

Gabriela Ivens, Human Rights Watch

Felim McMahon, Human Rights Center, University of California, Berkeley, School of Law

Daragh Murray, University of Essex

Yvonne Ng, WITNESS

Zara Rahman, The Engine Room

Mark Robson, Commission for International Justice and Accountability

Justin Seitz, Hunchly

Andrea Trewinnard, Human Rights Center, University of California, Berkeley, School of Law

Steve Trush, Center for Long-Term Cybersecurity, University of California, Berkeley

Raquel Vázquez Llorente, eyeWitness to Atrocities

Special acknowledgement

A special thank you to the members of the Online Investigations Working Group, Office of the Prosecutor, International Criminal Court.

Also acknowledged are the many colleagues within OHCHR whose efforts led to the realization of this joint publication.*

* In accordance with OHCHR policy, contributions to its publications are not attributed to those employed by the Office.

Abbreviations and acronyms

HTML	Hypertext Markup Language
ICRC	International Committee of the Red Cross
ICT	information and communications technology
IP	Internet Protocol
ISP	Internet service provider
NGO	non-governmental organization
OHCHR	Office of the United Nations High Commissioner for Human Rights
PDF	Portable Document Format
URI	uniform resource identifier
URL	uniform resource locator
VPN	virtual private network

1

INTRODUCTION

CHAPTER SUMMARY

- Purpose
- Audience
- Definitions

1. The Berkeley Protocol on Digital Open Source Investigations describes the professional standards that should be applied in the identification, collection, preservation, analysis and presentation of digital open source information and its use in international criminal and human rights investigations. Open source information is information that any member of the public can observe, purchase or request, without requiring special legal status or unauthorized access. Digital open source information is publicly available information in digital format, which is generally acquired from the Internet. Digital open source information comprises both user-generated and machine-generated data, and may include, for example: content posted on social media; documents, images, videos and audio recordings on websites and information-sharing platforms; satellite imagery; and government-published data.[1] Digital open source investigations are investigations based on digital open source information. For ease of reading, the Protocol will henceforth refer to digital open source information and investigations as "open source information" and "open source investigations", respectively.

2. While the use of open source information in investigations is not new, the volume and diversity of open sources have broadened as a result of the ever-increasing use of the Internet and other digital resources for information-sharing, including the proliferation of social media. The Protocol addresses both the complexities that arise when dealing with digital information and the unique challenges that come with evaluating sources and verifying information found on open online forums.

3. While a growing number of international criminal and human rights investigators now use the Internet to facilitate their work, no universal references, guidelines or standards for open source investigations currently exist. The Protocol seeks to fill that gap by setting out principles and practices that will help investigators conduct their work to a professional standard and facilitate, where appropriate, the preservation of open source information for potential use by accountability mechanisms.

4. The Protocol has a specific focus on open source investigations conducted for the purposes of ensuring international justice and accountability, which broadly include: human rights documentation, preservation, evidence collection and fact-finding; investigations by commissions of inquiry and fact-finding missions;[2] other types of internationally mandated investigations and inquiries;[3] truth and reconciliation processes; civil litigation; and criminal trials, including international criminal proceedings. As open source investigations can contribute to different types of efforts to ensure accountability,[4] the methodology and documentation requirements outlined in the Protocol may be more rigorous than those traditionally employed in other fields, such as journalism and human rights advocacy. Whatever the purpose of their investigation, by adhering to the methodological principles

---

[1] This is not an exhaustive list.

[2] Commissions of inquiry and fact-finding missions are bodies that may be established by Governments or international organizations to inquire into various issues. Commissions of inquiry or fact-finding missions report findings of fact, draw legal conclusions and make recommendations. While the findings of international commissions of inquiry or fact-finding missions are not legally binding, they can be highly influential. However, in some jurisdictions, the findings of national commissions of inquiry may be binding. For further information on international commissions of inquiry and fact-finding missions, see Human Rights Council, "International commissions of inquiry, commissions on human rights, fact-finding missions and other investigations". Available at www.ohchr.org/EN/HRBodies/HRC/Pages/COIs.aspx.

[3] See, e.g., the report of the United Nations High Commissioner for Human Rights on the situation of human rights in the Bolivarian Republic of Venezuela (A/HRC/41/18), submitted pursuant to Human Rights Council resolution 39/1. See also Council resolution 41/2, in which the Council requested the High Commissioner to prepare a report on the situation of human rights in the Philippines.

[4] E.g., open source information was used by the independent international fact-finding mission on Myanmar, alongside first-hand sources and other information, in its verification process and its findings and conclusions. The final report of the fact-finding mission (A/HRC/42/50) was one factor that led to the establishment, by the Human Rights Council, of the Independent Investigative Mechanism for Myanmar, which was given a mandate to carry out judicial investigations. The fact-finding mission was also mandated to hand over its information, including the content of its open source investigations, to the Independent Investigative Mechanism for Myanmar. The reports of the fact-finding mission were also relied upon in the case filed before the International Court of Justice by the Gambia against Myanmar for the latter's violation of the Convention on the Prevention and Punishment of the Crime of Genocide. This demonstrates how information collected for one purpose might ultimately contribute to another legal accountability process.

outlined in the Protocol, which are designed around common legal standards, open source investigators will ensure the high quality of their work and maximize the potential use of the information collected in courts, tribunals and other processes to ensure accountability.

5.   In addition, the Protocol emphasizes standards for investigating violations of international law, including human rights violations, and violations of international criminal law, including war crimes, crimes against humanity and genocide. Moreover, the guidance provided by the Protocol can be applied to other types of investigations, including those for national or municipal courts.

6.   Ultimately, the Protocol is designed to assist open source investigators to conduct their work in accordance with a professional methodology that is broadly consistent with legal requirements and ethical norms. It is also intended to help diverse end users of the investigation process, including lawyers and judges and other decision makers, to better understand and evaluate open source investigation techniques. The Protocol is equally intended as a resource for experienced practitioners and a training and teaching tool for those who wish to learn how to conduct open source investigations of alleged violations of international law.[5]

A. Purpose

7.   While investigators have long relied on open source information, its systematic exploitation accelerated in the early to mid-twentieth century with a focus on extracting intelligence from foreign radio broadcasts and print newspapers.[6] With the introduction of the World Wide Web in the 1990s, followed by the popularization of social media and smartphones in the 2000s, the quantity and quality of open source information has changed dramatically. Today, any individual with a smartphone and access to the Internet can create and distribute digital content globally, albeit of varying quality, veracity and transparency. The growing volume of data and speed by which such data are transmitted and shared have created new opportunities for open source investigators to gather and analyse information about international crimes and human rights violations. At the same time, content creators can now spread disinformation and manipulate digital data with relative ease. The Protocol is an attempt to respond to this new environment and the complexity of dealing with such opportunities and challenges.

8.   Open source information is useful in all kinds of investigations, but it plays a particularly critical role in international criminal and human rights investigations. This is true for a number of reasons. First, internationally mandated investigations, including those conducted by United Nations commissions of inquiry and fact-finding missions, or those authorized by the International Criminal Court, are dependent on legal and political processes permitting the investigation to take place.[7] Thus, they are often conducted long after the events. Second, often, international investigations may not have access to the physical location at which the incidents under investigation took place, for example, due to a State's refusal to cooperate or grant access. Third, even if granted access to a region or territory, investigators may have limited physical access to the location in question or may be impeded from in situ investigations or in-person interviewing due to concerns about protection. Finally, most investigators will not have full law enforcement powers over the territories in which the alleged crimes or violations occurred, and thus may be unable to collect the necessary information. Even in cases in which there is State cooperation, cross-border evidence collection can be an arduous process, slowed down by cumbersome bureaucratic procedures. All of these factors

---

[5]   The Protocol also provides some templates for open source investigations, as well as a glossary (see chap. VIII below).

[6]   Nikita Mehandru and Alexa Koenig, "ICTs, social media, & the future of human rights", Duke Law & Technology Review, vol. 17, No. 1, p. 129.

[7]   Commissions of inquiry and fact-finding missions mandated by the United Nations have been established by, among others, the Security Council, the General Assembly, the Human Rights Council and the Secretary-General. For the International Criminal Court, the Office of the Prosecutor can launch investigations upon referrals by States parties or by the Security Council, or on its own initiative and with the judges' authorization.

demonstrate why open source investigation techniques, which can be carried out remotely and conducted contemporaneously as events take place, are both powerful and necessary.

9. The Protocol is aimed at a diverse group of investigators working in different contexts with varying mandates, investigative powers and resources. Therefore, it takes a flexible approach that does not foresee investigators conducting their work identically, but rather adapting methodologies as appropriate for each unique working environment. Moreover, since the technologies, tools and techniques that assist open source investigations are constantly evolving, the Protocol does not focus on specific tools, platforms, websites, software or sources, which are subject to change, but on the underlying principles and procedures that should guide open source investigations.

10. The Protocol is designed to standardize procedures and provide methodological guidance across disparate investigations, institutions and jurisdictions to assist open source investigators in understanding the importance of:

    (a) Tracing the provenance of online content and attributing it to its original source, where possible;

    (b) Evaluating the credibility and reliability of online sources;

    (c) Verifying online content and assessing its veracity and reliability;

    (d) Complying with legal requirements and ethical norms;

    (e) Minimizing any risk of harm to themselves, their organizations and third parties;

    (f) Enhancing protection of the human rights of sources, including the right to privacy.

B. Audience

11. The target audience for the Protocol includes individuals and organizations that identify, collect, preserve and/or analyse open source

information in order to investigate international crimes or human rights violations for the purposes of ensuring justice and accountability. This includes investigators, lawyers, archivists and analysts who work for international, regional and hybrid criminal tribunals; national war crimes units; commissions of inquiry; fact-finding missions; independent investigative mechanisms; international organizations; transitional justice mechanisms; and non-governmental organizations (NGOs). Others who could benefit are those working for diverse international and regional mechanisms that carry out judicial and quasi-judicial open source investigations into violations of international law.[8] The Protocol may also be instructive for digital first responders, such as community-based organizations and independent researchers who are often the first to publish findings based on open source information, and whose work often plays a key role in the establishment of other formally mandated open source investigations. The target audience also includes individuals and organizations who support victims in bringing civil claims against individual perpetrators or States. The Protocol can also generally assist those who draw factual or legal conclusions on the basis of open source investigations, allowing them to better assess the content of any open source investigations that they are relying upon or evaluating.

12. Other potential stakeholders may include web-based service providers, such as social media platforms, that store large volumes of data and can play a key role in data preservation, and developers who provide software to bolster open source investigation techniques and processes.

C. Definitions

13. In order to provide practical standards and guidance for open source investigations, investigators must have a common understanding of specific terms. In this section, the key terminology used throughout the

---

[8] See, e.g., the communications and visit reports of the special procedures of the Human Rights Council. Available at www.ohchr.org/en/hrbodies/sp/pages/welcomepage.aspx. See also the work of the Sanctions Committees created by the Security Council. Available at www.un.org/securitycouncil/content/repertoire/sanctions-and-other-committees.

Protocol is clarified, including distinctions between commonly conflated terms.[9]

1. Open source versus closed source information

14. Open source information encompasses publicly available information that any member of the public can observe, purchase or request without requiring special legal status or unauthorized access. Closed source information is information with restricted access or access that is protected by law,[10] but which may be obtained legally through private channels, such as judicial processes, or offered voluntarily. Despite its simple definition, determining what constitutes open source information is more complicated than it initially appears in the context of online content. On the Internet, there is a growing volume of data that has been made public without the consent of the owners, such as information that has been hacked, leaked, exposed by security vulnerabilities or posted by a third party without proper permissions. While this information is publicly available and, therefore, technically considered open source, there may nevertheless be legal and ethical restrictions on certain types of end use. Furthermore, digital information may be accessible to those with specialized technical skills and training who can gain access to networks and data inaccessible to, or unlikely to be accessed by, the average person.[11] One example is information that can only be acquired on the dark web – namely, that part of the Internet that is only accessible through certain software, such as the Tor browser.[12] While the dark web offers anonymity, which has made it an attractive place for illegal activity, using the Tor browser and searching the dark web is legal in most countries. The Protocol includes this information within the realm of "open source" so long as there is no unauthorized access to

information. The clearest distinction is that open source information does not involve interacting with or soliciting information from individual Internet users.[13] Acquiring information from other Internet users through communication with those users is considered closed source.

15. Digital open source information[14] is open source information on the Internet, which can be accessed, for example, on public websites, Internet databases or social media platforms. The following are different ways of obtaining open source information.

2. Obtaining digital open source information

(a) Observation

16. Content on many platforms is obtainable simply by navigating to a relevant site using any number of free web browsers. Other online platforms require users to log in or register in order to access and view content. Such content is considered open source as long as those processes are open to all users in jurisdictions in which access is legal, and no privacy or security controls are breached when accessing or viewing it. However, some content that meets this definition may not be considered as open source, examples include privileged, classified or otherwise legally protected information. In such cases, while the information is observable by any member of the public, its use as evidence in judicial proceedings may be restricted. There may also be ethical or methodological concerns with relying on such material, such as the inability to attribute or verify that content.

(b) Purchase

17. Several sources of data for open source investigations are on platforms that require

---

[9]   For a more thorough compilation of relevant terms and definitions, see chap. VIII.

[10] E.g., privileged information and classified information.

[11] Some actions may breach a website's terms of service, but are not illegal per se. E.g., violating a website's terms of service to scrape data is unauthorized conduct and may result in being barred from using the website.

[12] The dark web refers to that part of the Internet that can only be accessed through specialized software. The Tor browser is one example of such software.

[13] While purchasing information from a private database or submitting a request for information from a public government agency require some degree of online exchange, it is often an automated process and is distinct from the type of interaction with other individual Internet users described here.

[14] Open source information may also be referred to as online content, online material or online data in the Protocol.

payment, or a combined free and premium model in which extra functionality and access to data comes with a financial cost. There are a growing number of businesses that aggregate public data and offer both free and paid services to access that data. Much information that open source investigators will find useful exists in databases and on platforms only accessible behind paywalls. For the purposes of the Protocol, open source information includes paid services that are available to all members of the public, but not services that limit access to certain groups, such as law enforcement personnel or licensed private investigators.

(c) Request

18. In this context, the term "request" refers to requests that can be made by any individual for public information from State agencies under freedom of information or access to information laws. It does not refer to requests to individuals, companies or organizations to voluntarily hand over their information, but is limited to requests to State entities that have legal obligations to respond in the same way to all persons. Open source investigations may lead to other online investigative activities, such as engagement with external sources using messaging services, chat rooms, forums or email. Such engagement is beyond the scope of open source investigation addressed in the Protocol.

3. Open source intelligence

19. Open source intelligence refers to a subcategory of open source information that is collected and used for the specific purpose of aiding policymaking and decision-making, most often in a military or political context. While open source information includes all publicly available information that anyone can lawfully obtain, open source intelligence is a subset of that information "that is collected, exploited, and disseminated in a timely manner to an appropriate audience for the purpose of addressing a specific intelligence requirement".[15] In the context of international criminal and human rights cases, open source intelligence is used as background information for decision-making functions – for example, to inform security-related activities, such as protecting witnesses and team members who go into the field or tracking persons of interest – rather than information-gathering functions related to investigation processes, such as establishing the elements of various crimes.

4. Open source investigation

20. Open source investigation refers to the use of open source information for information- and evidence-gathering functions.

5. Open source evidence

21. The term "evidence" should be distinguished from "information".[16] Evidence is generally defined across jurisdictions as proof of fact(s) used in an investigation or presented at a judicial hearing, such as a trial. Open source evidence is open source information with evidentiary value that may be admitted in order to establish facts in legal proceedings. It is important not to misuse or overuse the term "evidence" when referring to "information" generally.

---

[15] National Open Source Enterprise, Intelligence Community Directive No. 301, 11 July 2006, p. 8 (footnote omitted).

[16] Federica D'Alessandra and others, eds., *Handbook on Civil Society Documentation of Serious Human Rights Violations: Principles & Best Practices* (The Hague, Public International Law and Policy Group, 2016), p. 17.

6. Open source information versus open-source software

22. The term "open-source" is often used to describe software or code that is freely available to use and republish, without restrictions from copyright, patents or other legal controls. Open-source software is built from source code that anyone with access can inspect, modify and enhance.[17] It is usually not visible to users but can be adjusted and adapted by a computer programmer. Open-source software is distinguishable from open source information – although open-source software and tools are frequently used by open source investigators to find, collect, preserve and analyse open source information.

7. Credibility versus reliability

23. When it comes to testimonial evidence in international criminal trials, judges assess the "credibility of the witness" and the "reliability of his or her testimony".[18] In investigations by United Nations commissions of inquiry and fact-finding missions and similar investigations, guidance provides that "the interviewer should assess the interviewee's credibility and reliability".[19] The guidance elaborates that "the evaluation will consider the relevance of the information to the subject matter of the investigation. It will also look at the reliability of the source and the validity or truthfulness of the information."[20] The Protocol uses these terms as follows:

(a) "Credibility" refers to believability or trustworthiness;

(b) "Reliability" refers to the ability to perform consistently, dependably or as expected;

(c) "Veracity" or "validity" refers to accuracy, truthfulness or conformity with facts.

---

[17] See Opensource.com, "What is open source?".

[18] International Criminal Court, *Prosecutor v. Bosco Ntaganda*, Case No. ICC-01/04-02/06, Judgment of 8 July 2019, para. 53.

[19] OHCHR, *Commissions of Inquiry and Fact-Finding Missions on International Human Rights and Humanitarian Law: Guidance and Practice* (New York and Geneva, 2015), p. 52. Available at www.ohchr.org/Documents/Publications/CoI_Guidance_and_Practice.pdf.

[20] Ibid., p. 59.

PRINCIPLES

CHAPTER SUMMARY

- To comply with the professional principles related to digital open source investigations, investigators must ensure that they are accountable, competent and objective and that their work is carried out in accordance with the law and with due regard for security concerns.

- Investigators must also consider the methods that they use at all stages of the life cycle of their investigation. Relevant methodological principles include, at a minimum, accuracy, data minimization, data preservation and security by design.

- Finally, all investigators should be guided by ethical considerations. These include, at a minimum, protecting the dignity of all individuals who participate in or are implicated in an investigation, as well ensuring humility, inclusivity, independence and transparency.

24. While technologies, tools and techniques used in open source investigations will change, certain overarching methodological and ethical principles should endure. The identification of such principles is an important step towards professionalizing the field of open source investigations. The following principles are fundamental in ensuring the quality of open source investigations, which will, in turn, bolster their credibility, reliability and potential usefulness for the purpose of ensuring accountability and minimize potential harm to diverse stakeholders.

A. Professional principles

1. Accountability

25. Open source investigators must be accountable for their actions, which can often be ensured through clear documentation, record-keeping and oversight. Transparency in investigative methods and procedures is an essential element in ensuring accountability. Thus, to the extent possible and reasonable, open source investigators should maintain records of their activities. The steps of an open source investigation – from identification of relevant material through collection, analysis and reporting – should be consistently and clearly documented. Any individuals engaged in the collection or handling of online information should be aware of the potential for their methodology to be questioned, including the possibility of being called to testify at trial. Documentation of open source investigations may be done manually or by using automated processes provided by various software. As long as documentation is consistent and sufficiently thorough, either manual or automatic methods can be used. Automated processes and software must be understood by users and be explainable in court either by users or developers. In addition, open source investigators should record any tools or software used in the course of their work.

2. Competency

26. Open source investigators must have proper training and technical skills to execute the activities in which they engage. They must conduct online activities in a professional and ethical manner, avoiding the appropriation of others' work; crediting all those who participate in an investigation (when safe to do so and when desired by participants); and accurately reporting data, including acknowledging any gaps that may exist in online content. Open source investigators and investigation processes must also remain flexible, stay up to date with new developments and adopt new technologies and techniques as appropriate. In addition, organizations and investigation teams should have mechanisms in place to ensure that procedures are consistently implemented and adhered to.

3. Objectivity

27. Objectivity is a foundational principle that applies to all investigations, whether online or offline. Open source investigators should understand the potential for personal, cultural and structural biases to affect their work and the need to take countermeasures to ensure objectivity. Open source investigators must ensure that they approach their investigations objectively, developing and deploying multiple working hypotheses and not favouring any particular theory to explain their cases. For open source investigations conducted online, objectivity is particularly important because of the way in which information on the Internet is structured and presented to users. The browser, search engine, search terms and syntax used may lead to very different results, even when the underlying query is the same. Inherent biases in the Internet's architecture and algorithms employed by search engines and websites can threaten the objectivity of search results.[21] Search results may also be influenced by a number of technical factors, including the device used and its location, and the user's prior search history and Internet activity. Open source investigators should counterbalance such biases by applying methodologies to ensure that search results are

---

[21] See Safiya Noble, *Algorithms of Oppression: How Search Engines Reinforce Racism* (New York, New York University Press, 2018); Virginia Eubanks, *Automating Inequality: How High-Tech Tools Profile, Police, and Punish the Poor* (New York, Picador, 2019).

as diverse as possible, for example, by running multiple search queries and using a variety of search engines and browsers.[22] Investigators should be aware that search results may also be influenced by other factors, including as a result of the discrepancy in the digital environment whereby online information may be unevenly available from certain groups or segments of society.[23] Finally, investigators should always strive to be aware of and correct for their own biases, which may be either conscious or subconscious.[24]

4. Legality

28. Open source investigations should comply with applicable laws, which means that investigators need to have a baseline understanding of the laws that apply to their work. In particular, investigators should be aware of data protection laws and the right to privacy, which is protected under international human rights law.[25] Even though information may be publicly available, it does not mean that there are no privacy implications in its collection and use. Open source investigators must consider the privacy implications of their actions, including a person's reasonable expectation of privacy in different digital spaces. Investigators should also be aware of the mosaic effect, whereby public data, even when anonymized, may become vulnerable to reidentification if enough data sets containing similar or complementary information are released or combined.[26] In addition, investigators should be aware that, in some jurisdictions, the ongoing and persistent monitoring of individuals online, or the systematic collection and long-term retention of personal data, may require additional permissions and safeguards due

---

[22] See, e.g., Paul Myers, "How to conduct discovery using open source methods", in *Digital Witness, Using Open Source Information for Human Rights Investigation, Documentation and Accountability*, Sam Dubberley, Alexa Koenig and Daragh Murray, eds. (Oxford, Oxford University Press, 2020) (discussing the ways in which the selection of search engines and search terms can bias the results of open source investigations).

[23] See, e.g., Alexa Koenig and Ulic Egan, "Hiding in plain site: using online open source information to investigate sexual violence and gender-based crimes", in *Technologies of Human Rights Representation*, James Dawes and Alexandra S. Moore, eds. (forthcoming) (discussing how a relative lack of access to smartphones by women and the use of coded language online by survivors of sexual and gender-based violence may reduce the quantity and accessibility of open source information related to such crimes – as well as how the prevalence of men in both technology-related positions and as war crimes investigators may negatively affect the likelihood that automated and/or manual detection processes will produce open source information related to gendered crimes). For further discussion of bias, see chap. II.C below on ethical principles and chap. V.B below on digital landscape assessment.

[24] See, e.g., Forensic Science Regulator, *Cognitive Bias Effects Relevant to Forensic Science Investigations*, FSR-G-217 (Birmingham, United Kingdom, 2015) (discussing various categories of cognitive bias that can negatively affect investigative quality, including expectation bias, confirmation bias, anchoring, contextual bias, and role and reconstruction effects); Wayne A. Wallace, *The Effect of Confirmation Bias on Criminal Investigative Decision Making* (Minneapolis, Walden University ScholarWorks, 2015) (explaining confirmation bias as a process by which investigators search for or believe information that supports their favoured theory of a case "while ignoring or excusing disconfirmatory evidence"); Michael Pittaro, "Implicit bias within the criminal justice system", Psychology Today, 21 November 2018 (discussing biases that can influence criminal investigations generally and suggesting known debiasing techniques); Jon S. Byrd, "Confirmation bias, ethics, and mistakes in forensics", Forensic Pathways, 21 March 2020 (discussing various cognitive and ethical errors that can distort forensic analysis, as well as techniques for avoiding those errors). See also Yvonne McDermott, Daragh Murray and Alexa Koenig, "Digital accountability symposium: whose stories get told, and by whom? Representativeness in open source human rights investigations", Opinio Juris, 19 December 2019 (discussing how the methods of open source investigations may negatively affect "the types of violations reported, the victims and witnesses who have the opportunity to have their voices heard, and how narratives of mass human rights violations are constructed"); and the project led by Yvonne McDermott entitled "The future of human rights investigations: using open source intelligence to transform the documentation and discovery of human rights violations".

[25] Article 12 of the Universal Declaration of Human Rights provides that no one shall be subjected to arbitrary interference with his or her privacy, family, home or correspondence, nor to attacks upon his or her honour and reputation. Everyone has the right to the protection of the law against such interference or attacks. The International Covenant on Civil and Political Rights provides in article 17 that no one shall be subjected to arbitrary or unlawful interference with his or her privacy, family, home or correspondence, nor to unlawful attacks on his or her honour and reputation. It also states, in article 17, that everyone has the right to the protection of the law against such interference or attacks.

[26] "The notion of a mosaic effect is derived from the mosaic theory of intelligence gathering, in which disparate pieces of information – although individually of limited utility – become significant when combined with other types of information (Pozen 2005). Applied to public use data, the concept of a mosaic effect suggests that even anonymized data, which may seem innocuous in isolation, may become vulnerable to re-identification if enough datasets containing similar or complementary information are released." See John Czajka and others, *Minimizing Disclosure Risk in HHS Open Data Initiatives* (Washington, D.C., Mathematica Policy Research, 2014), appendix E, p. E-7. Available at https://aspe.hhs.gov/system/files/pdf/77196/rpt_Disclosure.pdf. See also David E. Pozen, "The mosaic theory, national security, and the Freedom of Information Act", *Yale Law Journal*, vol. 115, No. 3 (December 2005), pp. 628–679

to the heightened privacy concerns raised by such activities.[27]

5. Security awareness

29. While security by design[28] addresses the architecture and infrastructure of an investigation and any collateral activities, the principle of security awareness focuses on considerations that individuals must take into account in the course of their work – in particular, awareness of their online behaviour. All individuals conducting investigations online should have basic operational security awareness to ensure that they minimize their digital trail and are aware of the potential risks. Organizations conducting open source investigations should ensure that their investigators are provided with information security training to understand the risks that they may face and have an understanding of the three core pillars of information security: (a) confidentiality (e.g. only allowing permitted users to access data); (b) integrity (ensuring data is not tampered with or otherwise altered by unauthorized users); and (c) availability (ensuring systems and data are available to authorized users when they need it). Training should also focus on the Internet's governance structure. Threat and risk assessments should be conducted before commencing online investigative activities and should be periodically reviewed and amended as necessary. Security is everyone's responsibility, not only the responsibility of information technology units or security risk managers.

B. Methodological principles

1. Accuracy

30. There is a methodological and ethical imperative to ensure the accuracy – and thus the quality – of investigations by only relying on credible materials. Open source investigators should seek to be as truthful and precise as possible in the course of their investigations and in the presentation of any results, especially when it comes to acknowledging weaknesses in the underlying data or the overall case. Accuracy is often improved through the use and testing of multiple working hypotheses and/or peer review, both of which can help minimize the chances of biased selection, interpretation and presentation of data. Analytical conclusions should not be exaggerated or overstated. The use of clear, objective, fact-based language and the avoidance of emotive language will protect the actual and perceived objectivity of an investigation and its results.

2. Data minimization

31. The principle of data minimization prescribes that digital information should only be collected and processed if it is: (a) justified for an articulable purpose; (b) necessary for achieving that purpose; and (c) proportional to the ability to fulfil that purpose.[29] In the context of open source investigations, online content should only be collected if it is relevant to a particular investigation. This principle favours itemized, manual collection over bulk, automated collection, while

---

[27] E.g., in the United Kingdom of Great Britain and Northern Ireland, the law dictates that "personal data processed for ... law enforcement purposes must be kept for no longer than is necessary for the purpose for which it is processed" (Chapter 12 of the Data Protection Act 2018, part 3, chap. 3, sect. 39 (1)). Under Regulation 2016/679 of the European Parliament and of the Council of 27 April 2016 on the protection of natural persons with regard to the processing of personal data and on the free movement of such data, and repealing Directive 95/46/EC (General Data Protection Regulation), personal data can only be collected for "specified, explicit and legitimate purposes", must be limited to information necessary for the purpose for which they are collected and should remain identifiable only for as long as necessary for the purposes of collection (arts. 5–6).

[28] See para. 33 below.

[29] The Protocol derived the principle of data minimization from the European Union's General Data Protection Regulation, but adapted it to fit the open source investigation context (see art. 5 of the Regulation).

noting that the latter may be appropriate in some cases. Applying this principle to the collection of online content will help avoid over-collection, which is important for several reasons. Over-collection – a particular concern when using automated collection processes – may create or exacerbate security vulnerabilities,[30] in particular if it leads to investigators being unaware of the types of information within their possession. Over-collection may also raise privacy and data protection concerns if an automated process does not discriminate according to the type of content. Finally, avoiding over-collection serves the practical purposes of minimizing storage costs and preventing downstream bottlenecks at various stages of the investigation cycle, such as review, analysis and, in the event that an investigation leads to legal proceedings, disclosure.

3. Preservation

32. It is just as important to prevent under-collection as it is to avoid over-collection of relevant information. This may be of particular concern in the context of online information, the permanence and availability of which is often precarious. The principle of preservation is designed to avoid under-collection so that relevant and potentially probative evidence is not lost. Social media platforms, for example, may remove content that violates their terms of service even if that content has potential value for investigators. Unless a timely preservation request is made to the platform or content is otherwise preserved by investigators, such information may be lost forever. In addition, users may choose to delete or edit their own content, making once public information unavailable. Furthermore, information on the Internet can be easily decontextualized, lost, erased or corrupted. If digital material is to remain accessible and usable for future accountability mechanisms, it needs to be actively and carefully preserved in both the short and long term.[31]

4. Security by design

33. The principle of security by design requires that, to the extent possible, digital information and online operations be secure by default. Organizations conducting online open source investigations should invest in and implement appropriate technical and structural measures to ensure that, by default, infrastructure – including hardware and software – is properly anonymized and non-attributable when investigators go online. All equipment should have up-to-date software to protect against malware, and appropriate privacy and security settings. Security measures should be in place before online investigative activities commence; they should be continuously monitored, updated and adjusted as needed. Investigators, investigation teams or organizations may want to arrange for ongoing testing, including penetration testing,[32] to ensure that their security systems work as designed.

C. Ethical principles

1. Dignity

34. Investigations should be conducted with an awareness of and sensitivity to any underlying dignity-related issues, especially those interests that are protected by international human rights law. For example, investigators should adhere to the principles of non-discrimination, which may affect what gets investigated and who does the investigating or is credited with the investigation, and integrate safeguards concerning the digital, physical and psychosocial security of witnesses, survivors, other investigators, those accused and others who may be negatively affected. Adherence to the principle of dignity may also affect what is shared publicly about an investigation, including in writing and in any visual materials – for example, not showing the full extent of suffering or violence if it is not necessary to do so. This principle ensures that human rights norms are a guiding set of standards for conducting ethical open source investigations.

---

[30] See chap. IV below on security for examples of security vulnerabilities.

[31] See chap. VI.D below on preservation for more details.

[32] A penetration test is a simulated cyberattack that has been authorized in order to test a system's security.

II. PRINCIPLES

2. Humility

35. Open source investigators should be humble, recognizing their own limitations and having an awareness of what they do not know. Proper understanding and interpretation of open source information may require specialized training or consultations with experts. Humility also means taking responsibility for errors. If investigators find that they have made an error, that error should be corrected or reported to those who can minimize the resulting harm. Ideally, there should be a mechanism to report errors and for corrections to be issued, especially for investigations that are public and widely distributed.

3. Inclusivity

36. Open source investigators must ensure that a range of perspectives and experiences are incorporated into investigations. Factors to consider that may influence the overall inclusivity of an online investigation include its geographic scope, the violations and/or international crimes being investigated and an awareness of the uneven nature of online information with respect to different segments of society.[33] Investigation teams should also be diverse, which includes having a gender balance. In addition, the principle of inclusivity, together with the principle of dignity, may affect the materials an investigator chooses to collect and use in an investigation and how they are presented to different audiences.

4. Independence

37. Open source investigators should protect themselves and their investigations from inappropriate influence. They should identify and avoid any real or perceived conflicts of interest and put in place safeguards to mitigate those conflicts that cannot be avoided. Transparency of process, methods and funding can help with assessments of independence and protect the actual and perceived independence of an investigation.

5. Transparency

38. While the principle of accountability requires transparency in an investigator's methods and results, the ethical principle of transparency refers to how open source investigators conduct themselves online and to the outside world. This means avoiding misrepresentation.[34] While anonymity and non-attribution – including the use of virtual identities[35] – can be important for security reasons, investigators should be aware of the potential negative ramifications of misrepresentation, such as damaging the reputation and credibility of an investigation, team or organization, or contaminating the information collected. Procuring information through misrepresentation may violate a targeted individual's right to privacy and/ or taint an investigation, especially if the misrepresentation is illegal in the relevant jurisdiction(s).

---

[33] See chap. V.B below on digital landscape assessment.

[34] E.g., by trying to join closed groups or make connections on social media under false pretences.

[35] For a discussion of virtual identities, see chap. IV.C below on infrastructure-related considerations.

LEGAL FRAMEWORK

CHAPTER SUMMARY

- Determining which laws apply is critical in deciding what to collect and the best ways to do so. This will vary depending on the identities of the investigators, the identities of their targets, the purpose of their investigations and the jurisdictions in which they, the targets, the data and the legal processes are located.

- Preserving digital material in a way that maintains its authenticity and documents the chain of custody will increase the likelihood that it can be admitted as evidence in court.

- Identifying the type of investigation and its end goal (e.g. criminal proceedings, civil litigation, transitional justice process etc.) will determine the evidentiary threshold to be applied.

- Violating an individual's right to privacy could lead to the exclusion of evidence.

39. Open source investigators must understand the legal frameworks in which they operate. This includes knowledge of the applicable bodies of law relevant to their investigations and the legal frameworks of the jurisdictions in which they conduct investigative activities. Knowledge of the substantive laws applicable to the investigations, including the elements of potential violations[36] or crimes, as well as modes of liability,[37] can lead to more focused investigations and will increase the likelihood that the information collected and any analytical conclusions drawn will be helpful in efforts to ensure justice and accountability. Similarly, knowledge of the procedural laws and rules of evidence in the relevant jurisdictions will allow investigators to conduct their work in a manner that is consistent with the requirements for using open source information in legal proceedings.

40. For international criminal investigations, the legal framework will be prescribed by the statutory instruments of the relevant tribunal, court or court system.[38] For internationally mandated investigations, such as commissions of inquiry, the mechanism establishing the investigation will prescribe, among other factors, the applicable bodies of law and the geographic and temporal scope of the investigation.[39] For other investigations, including those undertaken by NGOs, the investigating entity itself may identify its own legal framework.[40]

41. This chapter has been designed to help open source investigators better appreciate and understand the potential end uses of their work and adapt their investigative techniques accordingly. Since applicable laws vary according to the jurisdiction, type of investigation and investigative entity's legal authority, the following sections provide an overview of the main considerations in investigating potential violations of international law. It is recommended that, where feasible, investigators obtain expert legal advice from lawyers familiar with the relevant jurisdictions and subject matter.

---

[36] As an example, if investigating hate speech and incitement to violence, investigators should understand the type of conduct that reaches the high threshold of article 20 (2) of the International Covenant on Civil and Political Rights. See Rabat Plan of Action on the prohibition of advocacy of national, racial or religious hatred that constitutes incitement to discrimination, hostility or violence (A/HRC/22/17/Add.4, appendix), paras. 11 and 29, and its human rights-based threshold test, available in 32 languages. Available at www.ohchr.org/EN/Issues/FreedomOpinion/Articles19-20/Pages/Index.aspx. Concerning hate speech, see the United Nations Strategy and Plan of Action on Hate Speech (2019). Available at www.un.org/en/genocideprevention/hate-speech-strategy.shtml.

[37] In criminal law, perpetrators may be held liable based on a number of modes of liability, as defined by the relevant statute. Such modes of liability include direct and indirect perpetration, co-perpetration, aiding and abetting and command responsibility. See Jérôme de Hemptinne, Robert Roth and Elies van Sliedregt, eds., *Modes of Liability in International Criminal Law* (Cambridge, United Kingdom, Cambridge University Press, 2019).

[38] See, e.g., International Criminal Court, Rules of Procedure and Evidence (2013); International Tribunal for the Former Yugoslavia, Rules of Procedure and Evidence (8 July 2015); International Criminal Tribunal for Rwanda, Rules of Procedure and Evidence (13 May 2015); Residual Special Court for Sierra Leone, Rules of Procedure and Evidence (30 November 2018); Special Tribunal for Lebanon, Rules of Procedure and Evidence (10 April 2019); Extraordinary Chambers in the Courts of Cambodia, Internal Rules (3 August 2011).

[39] E.g., the independent international fact-finding mission on the Bolivarian Republic of Venezuela, which was established in September 2019, is mandated to investigate extrajudicial executions, enforced disappearances, arbitrary detentions and torture and other cruel, inhumane or degrading treatment since 2014 and to present a report on its findings to the Council (Human Rights Council resolution 42/25, para. 24). The Independent International Commission of Inquiry on the Syrian Arab Republic, which was established in 2011, is mandated to investigate all alleged violations of international human rights law since March 2011 in the Syrian Arab Republic, to establish the facts and circumstances that may amount to such violations and of the crimes perpetrated and, where possible, to identify those responsible (Human Rights Council resolution S-17/1, para. 13). The international team of experts sent to the Kasai region of the Democratic Republic of the Congo in 2017 was mandated to collect and preserve information concerning alleged human rights violations and abuses, and violations of international humanitarian law in the Kasai regions, and to forward to the judicial authorities of the Democratic Republic of the Congo the conclusions of this investigation (Human Rights Council resolution 35/33, para. 10).

[40] Some organizations, including NGOs, often have their own internal methodologies that require them to focus on a particular area of law, e.g. concerning torture or sexual and gender-based violence, which will also provide guidance on the focus of the investigations.

A. Public international law

42. The Protocol focuses on three categories of public international law with substantial overlap: international humanitarian law, international human rights law and international criminal law. The three categories are mutually reinforcing; indeed, the applicability of international humanitarian law and/or international criminal law does not exempt States from fulfilling their obligations under international human rights law. The following provides an overview of each area of practice, including sources of law and distinctions among the fields of practice so that open source investigators know which references should guide their work.

1. International humanitarian law

43. International humanitarian law or the "law of armed conflict" regulates the conduct of hostilities and resolves humanitarian issues that arise in the context of such conflicts, which may be international or non-international in nature.[41] International humanitarian law is triggered when an armed conflict starts and extends until peace is achieved, although these delineations are not always definite or straightforward.[42] The main sources of international humanitarian law are The Hague Conventions of 1899 and 1907,[43] the Geneva Conventions of 12 August 1949[44] and the Protocols Additional thereto of 1977,[45] as well as several treaties that regulate the use of certain types of weapons.[46] Customary law is also an important source of international humanitarian law, as it fills gaps left by treaties. Customary international humanitarian law is binding on all parties to a conflict and is particularly relevant for non-international armed conflicts as its related rules are more detailed than those of treaty-based international humanitarian law.[47] Until the early 1990s, the primary enforcement mechanisms for international humanitarian law were national military tribunals, where States held their own enlisted members and officers accountable.

---

[41] The distinction between international and non-international armed conflict is based on two factors: the structure and status of the parties involved. International armed conflicts involve sovereign States. In contrast, non-international armed conflicts involve States and organized armed groups. See Andrew Clapham, Paola Gaeta and Marco Sassòli, eds., *The 1949 Geneva Conventions, A Commentary* (Oxford, Oxford University Press, 2015), chaps. 1 and 19.

[42] While the start of an international conflict is relatively clear, as it is triggered by any use of force between two States, the start of a non-international armed conflict is less straightforward. Non-international armed conflicts only exist if armed groups are sufficiently organized and the level of violence reaches a certain intensity – two factors that require detailed factual analysis on a case-by-case basis. See Sylvain Vité, "Typology of armed conflicts in international humanitarian law: legal concepts and actual situations", *International Review of the Red Cross*, vol. 91, No. 873 (March 2009), pp. 72 and 76–77. There is also contention regarding when an armed conflict ends and peace is achieved. While ceasefire or peace agreements may help demonstrate the end of an armed conflict, they are not dispositive. Various tests have been proposed for the end of an armed conflict, namely the general close of military operations once a general conclusion of peace is reached, the existence of a peaceful settlement and cessation of the criteria for identifying a conflict's existence. See Nathalie Weizmann, "The end of armed conflict, the end of participation in armed conflict, and the end of hostilities: implications for the detention operations under the 2001 AUMF", *Columbia Human Rights Law Review*, vol. 47, No. 3 (2016), pp. 221–224.

[43] Respectively, Convention with Respect to the Laws and Customs of War on Land (The Hague Convention II) and Convention respecting the Laws and Customs of War on Land (The Hague Convention IV).

[44] See Geneva Convention for the Amelioration of the Condition of the Wounded and Sick in Armed Forces in the Field (Geneva Convention I); Geneva Convention for the Amelioration of the Condition of Wounded, Sick and Shipwrecked Members of Armed Forces at Sea (Geneva Convention II); Geneva Convention relative to the Treatment of Prisoners of War (Geneva Convention III); Geneva Convention relative to the Protection of Civilian Persons in Time of War (Geneva Convention IV).

[45] See Protocol Additional to the 1949 Geneva Conventions of 12 August 1949, and relating to the Protection of Victims of International Armed Conflicts (Protocol I); Protocol Additional to the Geneva Conventions of 12 August 1949, and relating to the Protection of Victims of Non-International Armed Conflicts (Protocol II).

[46] See, e.g., Convention on the Prohibition of the Development, Production and Stockpiling of Bacteriological (Biological) and Toxin Weapons and on Their Destruction; Convention on Prohibitions or Restrictions on the Use of Certain Conventional Weapons Which May Be Deemed to Be Excessively Injurious or to Have Indiscriminate Effects; Convention on the Prohibition of the Development, Production, Stockpiling and Use of Chemical Weapons and on Their Destruction; Convention on the Prohibition of the Use, Stockpiling, Production and Transfer of Anti-Personnel Mines and on Their Destruction; Convention on Cluster Munitions. See also International Committee of the Red Cross (ICRC), "Weapons", 30 November 2011. Available at www.icrc.org/en/document/weapons.

[47] See ICRC, "Customary international humanitarian law", 29 October 2010. Available at www.icrc.org/en/document/customary-international-humanitarian-law-0. See also ICRC, "Welcome to the Customary IHL Database". Available at https://ihl-databases.icrc.org/customary-ihl/eng/docs/home.

With the rise of international criminal tribunals, certain serious violations of international humanitarian law were codified within the tribunals' founding statutes as war crimes,[48] providing a new avenue for enforcement of international humanitarian law at the international level. Some States have also codified war crimes in their national legislation,[49] so that such cases may be tried within their regular court systems, as opposed to military courts. National cases may take place in the country of the conflict or increasingly in other countries under the principle of universal jurisdiction.[50] A number of States have established specialized war crimes units to prosecute such cases. International criminal tribunals and national courts contribute to the growing body of jurisprudence on international humanitarian law, which also serves as an important source of law, the rules of which may be binding depending on the jurisdiction.

2. International human rights law

44. States have obligations and duties under international law to respect, protect and fulfil human rights. The Universal Declaration of Human Rights, adopted in 1948, provides the foundation of international human rights law. While it is aspirational and not legally binding, some of its articles form part of customary international law.[51] It has also inspired two covenants, and a rich body of human rights treaties.[52] States are only bound by those covenants and treaties that they have signed and ratified, unless the norms contained in those documents have attained the status of customary international law.[53] International human rights law has also been integrated into the statutory framework of many international criminal tribunals. In addition, there are several regional human rights courts established by international conventions with mandates to adjudicate cases against States parties to those conventions for violations of international human rights law, including the African Court on Human and Peoples' Rights,[54] the European Court of Human Rights[55] and the Inter-American Court of Human Rights.[56] There are additional human rights bodies at the regional level, including the African Commission on Human and Peoples' Rights, the European Committee of Social Rights and the Inter-

---

[48] E.g., article 8 of the Rome Statute of the International Criminal Court codifies international humanitarian law in its definition of war crimes.

[49] See, e.g.: Australia (War Crimes Act 1945, as amended, sect. 7); Bosnia and Herzegovina (Criminal Code, arts. 171–184); Kenya (International Crimes Act 2008, sect. 6 (1) (c) and (2)–(4)); New Zealand (International Crimes and International Criminal Court Act 2000, sect. 11); South Africa (Implementation of the Geneva Conventions Act 2012).

[50] Under "universal jurisdiction", a national court may prosecute individuals for serious crimes against international law – such as crimes against humanity, war crimes, genocide and torture – that took place outside the State's borders, based on the principle that such crimes harm the international community and international order itself, which individual States may act to protect. See International Justice Resource Center, "Universal jurisdiction". Available at https://ijrcenter.org/cases-before-national-courts/domestic-exercise-of-universal-jurisdiction.

[51] Numerous countries, United Nations officials and scholars have stated that the majority of the articles in the Universal Declaration of Human Rights, if not all of them, constitute customary international law. Specifically, the prohibitions against slavery, arbitrary deprivation of life, torture, arbitrary detention and racial discrimination codified in the Universal Declaration of Human Rights are accepted as constituting customary international law. See Hurst Hannum, "The status of the Universal Declaration of Human Rights in national and international law", *Georgia Journal of International and Comparative Law*, vol. 25, No. 1 (1996), pp. 322–332 and 341–346.

[52] See International Convention on the Elimination of All Forms of Racial Discrimination; International Covenant on Civil and Political Rights; International Covenant on Economic, Social and Cultural Rights; Convention on the Elimination of All Forms of Discrimination against Women; Convention against Torture and Other Cruel, Inhuman or Degrading Treatment or Punishment; Convention on the Rights of the Child. For further information on the core United Nations human rights treaties, see OHCHR, "The core international human rights instruments and their monitoring". Available at www.ohchr.org/EN/ProfessionalInterest/Pages/CoreInstruments.aspx.

[53] Customary international law refers to international obligations arising from established international practices, as opposed to obligations arising from formal written conventions and treaties. It results from a general and consistent practice of States that they follow from a sense of legal obligation. A fundamental component of customary international law is jus cogens, which refers to certain fundamental, overriding principles of international law. See, e.g., Legal Information Institute, "Customary international law" and "Jus cogens", Cornell Law School. Available at www.law.cornell.edu/wex.

[54] Established pursuant to the African Charter on Human and Peoples' Rights (Banjul Charter).

[55] Established pursuant to the Convention for the Protection of Human Rights and Fundamental Freedoms (European Convention on Human Rights).

[56] Established pursuant to the American Convention on Human Rights (Pact of San José).

American Commission on Human Rights, all of which continue to develop jurisprudence on international human rights law.

45. International organizations also play a key role in the development and standard setting of customary international human rights law.[57] The Office of the United Nations High Commissioner for Human Rights (OHCHR), as well as other international entities, publish thematic reports on areas of law that contribute to standard setting and soft-law development. The human rights treaty bodies[58] produce reports,[59] case law[60] and other forms of guidance, including general comments and general recommendations,[61] that contribute to the development and understanding of the articles of their respective treaties. Similarly, the special procedures of the Human Rights Council play a role in the evolution of standard-setting norms in international human rights law,[62] as do other mechanisms, including fact-finding missions and commissions of inquiry.

46. Similar to international humanitarian law, international human rights law has become part of the legal framework of many countries, either as a result of monistic legal traditions that directly apply international obligations in the national sphere or through the direct integration of international law into national legislation or through the application of universal jurisdiction, thereby developing important jurisprudence regarding such law.[63]

3. International criminal law

47. International criminal law applies both in times of peace and during armed conflict, imposing criminal liability on individuals who commit crimes under international law, including war crimes, crimes against humanity and genocide.[64] These crimes are sometimes collectively referred to as "atrocity crimes"[65] or "serious international crimes" and have been largely codified in the Rome Statute, which is broadly considered to reflect customary international criminal law. International criminal law also includes some crimes that are not codified in the

---

[57] Examples of international organizations include the International Criminal Court, the International Organization for Migration and the Organization for the Prohibition of Chemical Weapons, as well as human rights mechanisms, such as the special procedures and commissions of inquiry of the Human Rights Council or their equivalent. Special procedures exercise their mandates in relation to all States Members of the United Nations; they do not depend on ratification of a particular treaty. There are differences in the legal norms and the machinery of these human rights mechanisms, as well as differences in the methods and standards for collecting information. E.g., the primary working method of the Working Group on Arbitrary Detention is to receive information from the individuals concerned, their families or representatives, Governments, NGOs and national institutions about individual cases. The Working Group then investigates cases reported in communications, including through country visits. See A/HRC/36/38 for the latest methods of work of the Working Group. Commissions of inquiry, in contrast, are established by the Human Rights Council on an ad hoc basis, and typically initiate their own investigations in accordance with the terms of their mandates, often through country visits, during which they, among other things, conduct witness interviews. See, e.g., the terms of reference of the Commission of Inquiry on Burundi. Available at www.ohchr.org/Documents/HRBodies/HRCouncil/ColBurundi/TermsofreferenceCOIBurundiENGL.pdf.

[58] See, e.g., OHCHR, "Human rights treaty bodies". Available at www.ohchr.org/EN/HRBodies/Pages/TreatyBodies.aspx.

[59] Reports can be in the form of concluding observations, whereby a treaty body considers reports submitted by States parties and other stakeholders regarding implementation of the States' obligations under a particular treaty. Some treaty bodies are also able to issue reports on inquiries. See, e.g., Committee on the Elimination of Discrimination against Women, "Inquiry procedure". Available at www.ohchr.org/EN/HRBodies/CEDAW/Pages/InquiryProcedure.aspx.

[60] Treaty bodies issue Views on individual complaints in response to particular cases. See, generally, OHCHR, "Human rights treaty bodies – individual communications". Available at www.ohchr.org/EN/HRBodies/TBPetitions/Pages/IndividualCommunications.aspx#proceduregenerale.

[61] See OHCHR, "Human rights treaty bodies – general comments". Available at www.ohchr.org/EN/HRBodies/Pages/TBGeneralComments.aspx.

[62] See, generally, OHCHR, "Special procedures of the Human Rights Council". Available at www.ohchr.org/en/HRBodies/SP/Pages/Welcomepage.aspx.

[63] Amnesty International, *Universal Jurisdiction: A Preliminary Survey of Legislation Around the World – 2012 Update* (London, 2012), pp. 1–2.

[64] Robert Cryer, Darryl Robinson and Sergey Vasiliev, *An Introduction to International Criminal Law and Procedure*, 4th ed. (Cambridge, United Kingdom, Cambridge University Press, 2019), chap. 15.

[65] Although the term "ethnic cleansing" is not included in the Rome Statute, and is not defined as an independent crime under international law, it has been considered as belonging to the category of "atrocity crimes". In this context, please see United Nations, "Framework of analysis for atrocity crimes: a tool for prevention", p. 1. Available at www.un.org/en/genocideprevention/documents/about-us/Doc.3_Framework%20of%20Analysis%20for%20Atrocity%20Crimes_EN.pdf.

Rome Statute, such as terrorism.[66] There may be some overlap between international criminal law and the related field of transnational criminal law, which criminalizes cross-border acts such as trafficking in persons, drugs, weapons and other illicit goods.[67] In contrast to international humanitarian law and international human rights law, the focus of international criminal law is on individual criminal accountability rather than State responsibility. International criminal law cases may be tried in national criminal courts, hybrid criminal tribunals,[68] international criminal courts or tribunals,[69] including the International Criminal Court, or domestic courts exercising universal jurisdiction. Sources of international criminal law include the constituent documents of courts and tribunals (e.g. Security Council resolutions, statutes, rules of procedure and evidence, and regulations of the courts) and the national legislation of States that exercise jurisdiction over international crimes. Another important source of international criminal law is case law, which can be binding or persuasive depending on the jurisdiction.[70]

B. Jurisdiction and accountability

48. Jurisdiction is a legal term that refers to the authority granted to a legal entity, such as a court or tribunal, to prescribe, adjudicate and enforce a law. Justice and accountability are defined broadly in the Protocol to refer to different types of judicial and non-judicial processes. Accountability for international crimes and violations of international human rights law and/or international humanitarian law may result from legal proceedings, which may be criminal, civil or administrative in nature, as well as from non-legally binding processes, such as the reports of international human rights investigations, including commissions of inquiry and fact-finding missions, and other transitional justice mechanisms, including initiatives that focus on truth seeking. Investigators should strive, where possible, to take into account the range of possible jurisdictions in which accountability may be sought.

49. Open source investigators should identify the accountability mechanisms that may be relevant to their work and the potential venues where the evidence collected could or might be admitted to establish facts. However, at the early stages of international investigations these may be unknown or unclear. This is particularly true if the State in which the crimes were committed does not have a functioning judicial system or when the international community is not yet fully seized to investigate the matter. Moreover, it may not be possible to predict all jurisdictions that may be relevant in the future. When open source investigators do not know the specific mechanism or jurisdiction, they should strive to collect and preserve information in a way that maximizes its use in the widest range of potentially relevant jurisdictions. If investigators are aware of the relevant requirements for the venue in which the case will ultimately be tried, they should adapt their processes to those specific requirements.

50. Jurisdiction can be established in the following ways:

(a) Territorial jurisdiction is the authority of a court to hear cases relating to actions occurring in a defined territory. For international tribunals, territorial jurisdiction is usually limited to the territories of the States that have ratified the founding treaty;

(b) Temporal jurisdiction is the authority of a court to hear cases in which the alleged acts occurred during a prescribed time period;

---

[66] See Security Council resolution 1757 (2007), annex, Attachment (Statute of the Special Tribunal for Lebanon), art. 2.

[67] Cryer, Robinson and Vasiliev, *An Introduction to International Criminal Law and Procedure*, chap. 15.

[68] This term includes, inter alia, the Extraordinary Chambers in the Courts of Cambodia, the Special Court for Sierra Leone, the Special Tribunal for Lebanon, the Kosovo Specialist Chambers and Prosecutor's Office and the Special Criminal Court of the Central African Republic.

[69] This term includes the permanent International Criminal Court and the ad hoc International Tribunal for the Former Yugoslavia, the International Criminal Tribunal for Rwanda and the International Residual Mechanism for International Criminal Tribunals.

[70] See Rosa Theofanis, "The doctrine of res judicata in international criminal law", *International Criminal Law Review*, vol. 3, No. 3 (2003).

(c) Personal jurisdiction is the authority of a court to make decisions regarding a party to the proceedings;

(d) Subject matter jurisdiction is the authority of a court to hear cases of a particular type or cases relating to a specific subject matter;

(e) Universal jurisdiction is the claim of authority by a court over an accused person regardless of where the alleged crime was committed, and regardless of the accused's nationality, country of residence or any other relation with the prosecuting entity.

C. Investigative powers and duties

51. Formal investigative powers are those vested by law in a specific entity to investigate within a given jurisdiction. Much like the limits on judicial authority, a judicial or prosecutorial entity can only conduct investigations to the extent that they are authorized to do so by law.[71] Investigative powers may include the ability to compel witnesses, subpoena records and execute search warrants. An investigative entity may be required by law to follow strict procedures or in some instances may be able to determine its own procedures.[72]

52. Most others investigating violations of international law will generally not be vested with investigative powers or enforceable means of evidence collection, such as subpoenas or search warrants. Thus, they may be wholly reliant on open source information and information provided voluntarily, such as documents, digital files and witness testimony.

53. Generally, investigative powers are accompanied by delineated duties.[73] Although some investigators may not have police powers or other legal authority, it is recommended, to the extent possible, that all investigators seek to comply with the key duties of legal investigators, in order to ensure the quality of investigations. Common duties and obligations of legal investigators and prosecutors include the duty to investigate incriminating and exonerating circumstances, the duty to protect witnesses, the duty to preserve evidence, the duty to ensure the fairness of proceedings and the obligation to respect the rights of accused persons.

54. In criminal trials, prosecutors are also obligated to disclose relevant information and evidence to the defence.[74] This includes more than just the evidence admitted at trial, but any information gathered as part of an investigation that is incriminating or exonerating, including information related to the credibility of witnesses.[75] There are certain exceptions related to privileged information or information that could place a person at risk. A court may order the non-disclosure of the identity of a victim or witness who may be endangered by such a disclosure, but this is never guaranteed.[76] Many criminal jurisdictions have disclosure rules that require prosecutors to turn over

---

[71] See Justia, "Agency investigations". Available at www.justia.com/administrative-law/agency-investigations.

[72] Ibid.

[73] E.g., article 54 of the Rome Statute delineates the duties and powers of the Prosecutor with respect to investigations, establishing the Prosecutor's ability, inter alia, to conduct investigations, collect and examine evidence, interview victims and witnesses and cooperate with States and international organizations.

[74] See, e.g., International Tribunal for the Former Yugoslavia, Rules of Procedure and Evidence, rule 66 (A); International Criminal Tribunal for Rwanda, Rules of Procedure and Evidence, rule 66 (A); Special Tribunal for Lebanon, Rules of Procedure and Evidence, rule 110 (A).

[75] See, e.g., International Criminal Court, Rules of Procedure and Evidence, rules 76–84; International Tribunal for the Former Yugoslavia, Rules of Procedure and Evidence, rule 66 (A) (ii); International Criminal Tribunal for Rwanda, Rules of Procedure and Evidence, rule 66 (A) (ii); Special Court for Sierra Leone, Rules of Procedure and Evidence, rule 66 (A) (ii); Special Tribunal for Lebanon, Rules of Procedure and Evidence, rule 110 (A) (ii); Special Panels for Serious Crimes in East Timor, Transitional Rules of Criminal Procedure, sect. 24.4.

[76] See, e.g., International Criminal Court, Rules of Procedure and Evidence, rule 81 (4); International Tribunal for the Former Yugoslavia, Rules of Procedure and Evidence, rule 69; International Criminal Tribunal for Rwanda, Rules of Procedure and Evidence, rule 69; Special Court for Sierra Leone, Rules of Procedure and Evidence, rule 69; Special Tribunal for Lebanon, Rules of Procedure and Evidence, rules 115–116; Special Panels for Serious Crimes in East Timor, Transitional Rules of Criminal Procedure, sect. 24.6.

anything that is potentially exculpatory.[77] Open source investigators working on any case with even the slightest chance of it ending up in court should take these disclosure obligations into consideration when conducting their work.[78] There are several other reasons why investigators should consider the potential for disclosure of information. For example, if prosecutors are required to review all of the material collected in an investigation, investigators should be wary of collecting in bulk, as a high a volume of information may be overly burdensome or even impossible to review. This is also relevant when it comes to preservation and storage of the information collected, including proper tagging, which will provide significant benefit to those seeking to retrieve and review the material later.

D. Rules of procedure and evidence

55. When working in the context of a legal investigation, the main task of open source investigators is to collect information that is relevant and authentic so that it can be used to draw factual and legal conclusions. Particularly in international courts and tribunals, investigators must aim to ensure that any open

source evidence that is collected is admissible, as well as relevant, reliable and probative. Criminal investigations are distinguished from investigations conducted for other purposes by their higher applicable standard of proof[79] and more stringent rules of procedure and evidence, including admissibility, in order to protect the due process and fair trial rights of any accused persons.[80] While the bar for admissibility of evidence in international criminal courts and tribunals is generally lower than that of some national courts, the methods of evidence collection will still affect the weight judges give to the evidence. This is true in all jurisdictions. In an era marked by the proliferation of digital information, including both misinformation and disinformation,[81] it is crucial that investigators be able to determine whether open source information is authentic and establish or disprove its veracity with sufficient accuracy.[82]

56. For judicial proceedings, admissibility refers to whether an item submitted by a party to the proceedings may be admitted into the record as evidence. Generally, international criminal tribunals evaluate the admissibility of a proffered item using a three-factor test: (a) relevance; (b) probative value; and (c) probative value weighed against any prejudicial effect on the

---

77   See, e.g., International Tribunal for the Former Yugoslavia, Rules of Procedure and Evidence, rule 68; International Criminal Tribunal for Rwanda, Rules of Procedure and Evidence, rule 68; Special Court for Sierra Leone, Rules of Procedure and Evidence, rule 68; Special Tribunal for Lebanon, Rules of Procedure and Evidence, rule 113; Rome Statue of the International Criminal Court, art. 67 (2); Special Panels for Serious Crimes in East Timor, Rules of Procedure and Evidence, rule 24.4 (c). Exculpatory evidence is evidence that might exonerate a defendant. In the United States, the Brady doctrine is a pretrial discovery rule that was established by the United States Supreme Court, requiring that the prosecution turn over all exculpatory evidence to the defendant in a criminal case. See *Brady v. Maryland*, 378 U.S. 83 (1963).

78   Because disclosure obligations may require that some or all collected materials may have to be turned over to the defence, open source investigators' ability to protect identities and other sensitive information may be negated.

79   E.g., while international courts will usually apply the criminal law standard of proof "beyond reasonable doubt", commissions of inquiry and similar bodies have most commonly adopted the lower standard of "reasonable grounds to believe" upon which to base their findings. For further information, see OHCHR, *Commissions of Inquiry and Fact-Finding Missions on International Human Rights and Humanitarian Law: Guidance and Practice*, pp. 62–63.

80   International Criminal Court, *Prosecutor v. Jean-Pierre Bemba*, Case No. ICC-01/05-01/08 A, Judgment on the Appeal of Mr Jean-Pierre Bemba Gombo against Trial Chamber III's "Judgment pursuant to Article 74 of the Statute", 8 June 2018, Appeals Chamber, Separate Opinion of Judge Van den Wyngaert and Judge Morrison, para. 5.

81   Misinformation is information that is false, but not intended to cause harm. E.g., individuals who do not know a piece of information is false may spread it on social media in an attempt to be helpful. Disinformation is false information that is deliberately created or disseminated with the express purpose of causing harm. Producers of disinformation typically have political, financial, psychological or social motivations. See Claire Wardle, "Information disorder: the essential glossary" (Cambridge, Massachusetts, Shorenstein Center on Media, Politics and Public Policy, 2018). Available at https://firstdraftnews.org/wp-content/uploads/2018/07/infoDisorder_glossary.pdf?x32994.

82   Ibid.

fairness of the trial.[83] The item will be relevant if it helps make a fact more or less probable, while its probative value refers to whether the item helps prove or disprove a fact at issue in the case. In the case of non-judicial investigations, an assessment similar to admissibility is applied. Every piece of information should be assessed in terms of its reliability, relevance and probative value to determine if and how it should be used in the determination of legal and/or factual conclusions.[84]

57. Weight refers to the value attributed to an item and the degree to which it will ultimately be relied upon in drawing a legal or factual conclusion. The determination of weight should be a holistic assessment that depends, in part, on the other information that may support, corroborate or contradict the fact in question. In many legal proceedings, admissibility and weight are assessed separately. In other contexts, in situations in which admissibility of evidence is not a factor, human rights investigators will apply a similar approach in assessing the weight to be attributed to the information.

58. Rules of procedure and evidence applicable to international criminal proceedings can be found in each court's constituent instruments, most commonly their rules of procedure and

evidence. Case law provides further guidance. Depending on the nature of an investigation, it may be worth contacting a legal expert for advice. This is particularly true if an investigation is intended to contribute to court proceedings.

59. Open source information may be a combination of documentary and testimonial evidence. For example, a video of a person making statements will need to be authenticated and the statements made within will have to be verified separately.[85] Therefore, the means of authenticating the digital item as a document or assessing its reliability and admissibility as testimonial evidence may apply. Investigators should be aware of the ways in which each category of evidence is treated in the relevant jurisdiction. Documentary evidence may often be admitted even if the author is not known or unavailable to testify. It may also be admissible without having to introduce the document through a witness who can authenticate it, provided that the offering party can demonstrate with clarity and specificity where and how that document fits into the case.[86]

60. In situations in which responsibility for crimes and violations is attributed to those higher up the command structure, the information collected

---

83 Under the Rome Statute (arts. 64 (9) (a) and 69 (4)), the Trial Chamber of the International Criminal Court has "the power on application of a party or on its own motion to … rule on the admissibility or relevance of evidence … taking into account, inter alia, the probative value of the evidence and any prejudice that such evidence may cause to a fair trial or to a fair evaluation of the testimony of a witness, in accordance with the Rules of Procedure and Evidence."

84 See, e.g., OHCHR, *Commissions of Inquiry and Fact-Finding Missions on International Human Rights and Humanitarian Law: Guidance and Practice*, in particular chap. IV.C on gathering and assessing information.

85 See Human Rights Center, University of California, Berkeley, School of Law, "Digital fingerprints: using electronic evidence to advance prosecutions at the International Criminal Court (Berkeley, 2014). Available at www.law.berkeley.edu/files/HRC/Digital_fingerprints_interior_cover2.pdf. Hearsay evidence is information outside the direct knowledge of the testifying witness. In some jurisdictions, hearsay evidence is inadmissible unless it meets a specific exception. In others, it is admissible but given little weight due to the fact that it cannot be properly tested on cross-examination by either the prosecution or the defence. According to the Organization for Security and Cooperation in Europe, "while hearsay evidence is generally not admissible in common-law jurisdictions absent special circumstances there is no prohibition against hearsay evidence in civil law jurisdictions or in international tribunals". See Organization for Security and Cooperation in Europe, Mission to Bosnia and Herzegovina, *Investigation Manual for War Crimes, Crimes Against Humanity and Genocide in Bosnia and Herzegovina* (Sarajevo, 2013), p. 26. Available at www.osce.org/bih/281491?download=true. Despite this lack of barriers in civil law jurisdictions and international tribunals, as a general rule, hearsay evidence is viewed as a particularly unreliable category of indirect evidence and judges often give it relatively little weight.

86 See, e.g., International Tribunal for the Former Yugoslavia, *Prosecutor v. Pavle Strugar*, Case No. IT-01-42-T, Decision on the Admissibility of Certain Documents, 26 May 2004, Trial Chamber II, and *Prosecutor v. Milan Milutinović et al.*, Case No. IT-05-87-T, Decision on Prosecution Motion to Admit Documentary Evidence, 10 October 2006, Trial Chamber; International Criminal Tribunal for Rwanda, *Prosecutor v. Edouard Karemera et al.*, Case No. ICTR-98-44-T, Decision on Joseph Nzirorera's Motion to Admit Documents from the Bar Table: Public Statements and Minutes, 14 April 2009, Trial Chamber III; International Criminal Court, *Prosecutor v. Thomas Lubanga Dyilo*, Case No. ICC-01/04-01/06, Decision on the Admission of Material from the "Bar Table", 24 June 2009; International Tribunal for the Former Yugoslavia, *Prosecutor v. Radovan Karadžić*, Case No. IT-95-5/18-PT, Order on Prosecution Request for Clarification and Proposal concerning Guidelines for the Conduct of Trial, 20 October 2009, Trial Chamber, and *Prosecutor v. Radovan Karadžić*, Case No. IT-95-5/18-T, Decision on the Prosecution's First Bar Table Motion, 13 April 2010, Trial Chamber; International Criminal Court, *Prosecutor v. Germain Katanga and Mathieu Ngudjolo Chui*, Case No. ICC-01/04-01/07, Decision on the Prosecutor's Bar Table Motions, 17 December 2010, Trial Chamber II.

may be used not only to establish the "crime base" (see below) but may also be relevant in proving the mode of liability[87] of the alleged individual perpetrator(s).[88] Individuals may be considered responsible when each element of a crime or violation, including the physical acts (actus reus) and the accused's mental state (mens rea), is demonstrated to the applicable standard of proof. To make this determination, the fact finder will examine the information introduced with respect to each element of the violation or crime. Investigators should be familiar with which crimes or violations may be alleged, the elements of each, who is being accused of having perpetrated them and under which theory of liability. In international criminal law cases, practitioners often separate "crime-based evidence" from "linkage evidence". These two concepts are explained as follows:

(a) Crime-based evidence is evidence of the crimes upon which the charges are based, including information about who, what, where and when.[89] For example, if the alleged perpetrator is charged with murder as a crime against humanity, any information proving that there was a murder is considered crime-based evidence;

(b) Linkage evidence is evidence of the responsibility of the alleged perpetrator for the crimes committed, which is particularly important if the perpetrator did not directly commit the crime.[90] In other words, it is the evidence that connects the responsible party with the crime. For example, in cases in which the allegation is that a superior failed to prevent or punish alleged violations of which they were aware, linkage evidence is that which proves this awareness or the fact that the superior was in "effective control" of the direct perpetrator.

E. Right to privacy and data protection

61. The right to privacy is a fundamental human right.[91] An important element of the right to privacy is the right to the protection of personal data, which has been articulated in various data protection laws.[92] In particular, data protection and privacy laws are increasingly relevant in investigations that utilize digital information and communications technology (ICT). The following provides a brief overview of the concepts of the international human right to privacy and the global framework for data protection, data security and data sharing of which open source investigators should be aware. In the digital environment, informational privacy, covering information that exists or can be derived about a person, is of particular importance.[93]

62. Open source investigators must respect human rights and should be particularly sensitive to the right to privacy, which is frequently raised in the context of digital information. For example, a violation of the right to privacy is one of the few

---

[87] Cryer, Robinson and Vasiliev, *An Introduction to International Criminal Law and Procedure*, chap. 15.

[88] See OHCHR, *Who's Responsible? Attributing Individual Responsibility for Violations of International Human Rights and Humanitarian Law in United Nations Commissions of Inquiry, Fact-Finding Missions and Other Investigations* (New York and Geneva, 2018). Available at https://ohchr.org/Documents/Publications/AttributingIndividualResponsibility.pdf.

[89] Kelly Matheson, *Video as Evidence Field Guide* (WITNESS, 2016), p. 42. Available at https://vae.witness.org/video-as-evidence-field-guide.

[90] Ibid.

[91] The right to privacy is included in numerous human rights instruments and in the constitutional statutes of more than 130 countries. See, e.g., American Declaration of the Rights and Duties of Man, art. V; European Convention on Human Rights, art. 8; American Convention on Human Rights, art. 11; Convention on the Rights of the Child, art. 16; International Convention on the Protection of the Rights of All Migrant Workers and Members of Their Families, art. 14; African Charter on the Rights and Welfare of the Child, art. 10; Arab Charter on Human Rights, arts. 16 and 21; Association of Southeast Asian Nations Human Rights Declaration, art. 21. See also Privacy International, "What is privacy?", 23 October 2017. Available at https://privacyinternational.org/explainer/56/what-privacy.

[92] There are data protection laws in over 100 countries and in numerous international and regional instruments. See, e.g., Organization for Economic Cooperation and Development, Guidelines on the Protection of Privacy and Transborder Flows of Personal Data; Council of Europe, Convention for the Protection of Individuals with Regard to Automatic Processing of Personal Data; Charter of Fundamental Rights of the European Union; Asia-Pacific Economic Cooperation Privacy Framework; Supplementary Act on Personal Data Protection within the Economic Community of West African States.

[93] See, generally, A/HRC/39/29, para. 5.

grounds on which judges may exclude evidence at the International Criminal Court.[94] Privacy underpins and protects human dignity and other key values, such as freedom of association and freedom of expression. The European Court of Human Rights provides some of the strongest interpretations of privacy laws, with a quickly growing body of case law addressing digital rights issues. Violations of such fundamental rights will inevitably lead to challenges by the defence in criminal proceedings and could even result in civil causes of action against investigating parties. In addition to privacy laws, numerous data protection laws and regulations help ensure the security of personal data. In particular, open source investigators should be aware of Regulation 2016/679 of the European Parliament and of the Council of 27 April 2016 on the protection of natural persons with regard to the processing of personal data and on the free movement of such data, and repealing Directive 95/46/EC (General Data Protection Regulation), and its approach to individual data protection, because this law has set a high standard and other States are considering adopting similar legislation.[95] However, data protection regulations differ from country to country, with significant variations and even sometimes directly conflicting rules. Open source investigators should consult a legal expert in order to make themselves aware of the applicable data protection laws and regulations relevant to the jurisdictions in which they operate.

63. Finally, open source investigators should be aware of the general prohibition on the unauthorized access of data and networks. For example, this would include using a leaked password found in a breached data set to access restricted material, as well as gaining unauthorized access to restricted information through deception and other forms of social engineering.[96]

F. Other relevant legal considerations

64. In the course of open source investigations, other laws may be relevant. The following is a non-exhaustive list of some of the legal considerations of which open source investigators should be aware.

1. Violating terms of service

65. Some common open source investigation techniques involve breaches of the terms of service of a website or platform. For example, scraping data or using a virtual identity (not one's real identity) violates the terms of service of platforms and, in particular, social media platforms.[97] Violating the terms of service is a breach of contract. Investigators should verify whether it may also be an illegal act in the jurisdictions in which they are working. The need to uphold security principles that can be provided through the use of virtual identities must be balanced against potential harm for breach of contract in such circumstances, the most common remedy for which being the disabling of a user's access to a platform. However, while virtual identities are necessary when used for purely open source searching and monitoring, as noted above, virtual identities should not be used to try and access content shared on social media that is subject to restrictive access controls; or as a pretext to

---

[94] See Rome Statute, art. 69 (7).

[95] The Regulation states that natural persons have rights associated with the protection of personal data, the protection of the processing of personal data and the unrestricted movement of personal data within the European Union. Similar rights are also provided for in the Convention for the Protection of Individuals with Regard to Automatic Processing of Personal Data and notably the Protocol of 2018 thereto. The Convention binds not only Council of Europe member States but also a number of other States.

[96] According to the United States National Institute of Standards and Technology, social engineering is "the act of deceiving an individual into revealing sensitive information by associating with the individual to gain confidence and trust" (Paul A. Grassi, Michael E. Garcia and James L. Fenton, *Digital Identity Guidelines* (Gaithersburg, Maryland, National Institute of Standards and Technology, 2017), p. 54. See also Michael Workman, "Gaining access with social engineering: an empirical study of the threat", *Information Systems Security*, vol. 16, No. 6 (2007). For further discussion of unauthorized and deceptive access, see para. 65 below. For a discussion of user camouflage, see para. 107 below.

[97] E.g., Facebook's Terms of Service require users to "use the same name that you use in everyday life", to "provide accurate information about yourself" and to "create only one account (your own) and use your timeline for personal purposes". See www.facebook.com/terms.php. Impersonation violates Twitter's Rules and Policies. See "Impersonation policy" at https://help.twitter.com/en/rules-and-policies/twitter-impersonation-policy.

elicit information directly from a person under the pretences of a false identity. Such conduct would take investigators outside the realm of open source investigation, would violate ethical principles[98] and could breach the law.[99]

2. Intellectual property laws

66. Investigators should be aware of any intellectual property permissions that they may need to acquire to lawfully publish, distribute and/ or otherwise use information that they have collected during the course of an investigation. The relevant laws vary from jurisdiction to jurisdiction, although most jurisdictions provide (at a minimum) some form of copyright protection to the creator of a piece of content, such as a video, photograph or piece of text shared online. The "creator" is usually defined as the person who actually created the material – for example, by taking the picture, recording the video or writing the original text – and not the uploader, although they can be one and the same person. The end user may need to get the creator's consent for the proposed use in order to avoid a copyright violation (e.g. if using the content in a public report or journalistic story) – getting the uploader's consent, if that person is not also the creator, is usually not enough to avoid violating the law. This is yet another reason to try to locate the original source of each piece of content investigators may acquire. Some (but not all) jurisdictions provide exceptions to the need to acquire consent – often called "fair use" or "fair dealing" exceptions – when videos, photographs, text and other information are used for certain socially beneficial purposes, such as education, law enforcement or journalism. However, these exceptions, when applicable, are often quite narrow, and thus a particular use should never be assumed to fall within such an exception without a careful review. Mechanisms that can sometimes help minimize the likelihood and/ or scope of infringement include embedding a link to the original content in a digital report without removing it from its original source; crediting the creator; and using only a small portion of the original content – however, again, this is context and jurisdiction specific. Information subject to Creative Commons licences or other free licences may have a broad range of permissible uses at no cost. However, if such free licences apply, it is important to comply with the licence conditions and not treat the content as permission free.

---

[98] For a discussion of misrepresentation, see chap. II.C above on ethical principles.

[99] See chap. III.E above on the right to privacy and data protection.

SECURITY

CHAPTER SUMMARY

- Everyone is responsible for ensuring the security of an investigation and those affected by it, not just information technology professionals.

- Security considerations should be twofold: (a) related to infrastructure, including hardware, software and networks; and (b) related to behaviour, including that of the investigators and all those with whom they interact.

- Security assessments should be carried out at three levels, including at the level of the organization, specific investigation/case and specific activities/tasks.

- Protection measures should be designed to mitigate risks and threats, as identified in an investigation risk assessment.

- Security assessments should factor in all types of harms, including digital, financial, legal, physical, psychosocial and reputational harm.

- Some of the greatest vulnerabilities in open source investigations are associated with internet connections/IP addresses, devices and their features, and user behaviour.

- Investigators and investigating organizations should engage in ongoing security training and deploy protection measures that evolve with the changing nature of any threats or vulnerabilities.

67. This chapter contains an overview of online and offline security considerations related to open source investigations. With appropriate preparation, investment and focus on threat assessment and risk mitigation, open source investigators should be able to minimize the risk of harm to people, data and other assets. Security infrastructure, including hardware and software, and protocols for user behaviour should, to the extent possible, be put in place prior to beginning an investigation, evaluated regularly and updated as necessary. An organization's size and resources may have an impact on the feasibility of certain protection measures; therefore, this chapter contains flexible standards, which should be adapted according to the specific needs of an organization and an investigation. Organizations conducting high-risk investigations – such as investigations involving particularly vulnerable victims or in situations in which the alleged perpetrators are State actors and/or identified individually – should engage the services of experienced cybersecurity professionals. In addition, a robust security framework should include some kind of independent auditing mechanism and continuous training so that users can stay abreast of new technological developments and best practices.

A. Minimum standards

68. Since security infrastructure and best practices for user behaviour are constantly changing, the Protocol offers overarching principles to help guide open source investigators in thinking through security. Investigators must be responsible for their own security, including assessing the level of risk posed by their conduct and putting in place adequate risk mitigation and protection measures. Despite the need for a customized and individualized approach to security, there are some minimum standards that open source investigators should always apply to their work in order to comply with security principles:

(a) Open source investigators should avoid disclosing identifiable elements about themselves, their organizations and any partners or sources to third parties unless this is an investigative objective or obligation. Investigators should therefore maintain their anonymity online and ensure that their online activities are non-attributable to the greatest extent possible;

(b) Open source investigators should conduct online activities with the expectation that such activities may be monitored and analysed by third parties. Therefore, they should conduct online activities in a manner that is consistent with their virtual identities and in a way that does not reveal their identities or investigative objectives, or endanger their human sources or other third parties;

(c) Open source investigators should be aware that over-exploitation of a single online source of information, such as a specific site, may increase the risk of third-party monitoring and analysis. Therefore, they should put in place practices to minimize this likelihood, such as diversifying digital sources;

(d) Open source investigators should avoid identifiable or predictable patterns of behaviour, such as repetitive search patterns on identifiable devices, which might aid a third party's identification of the objectives of an investigation, as well as make investigators easier targets for phishing attacks and other forms of social engineering;[100]

(e) Open source investigators should keep their professional work separate from personal online activities. Personal online accounts and, to the extent possible, personal equipment should not be used for professional investigations and professional equipment should never be used for personal online activities;[101]

---

[100] See below for an explanation of phishing attacks and social engineering.

[101] If use of personal equipment is unavoidable, users should conduct professional investigations and personal activities in separate online environments, e.g. by using a virtual machine for their investigations.

(f) Open source investigators conducting multiple investigations should not intermingle their investigations. Therefore, they should keep different start and end times for each investigation activity, maintain data and documentation for each investigation in separate locations and use different virtual identities, as necessary;[102]

(g) Open source investigators should use technical systems or environments that are designed to be minimally affected by the possible introduction of hostile or malicious software or other disruptive influences that might be encountered during activities.

B. Security assessments

69. In order to develop an appropriate and effective security framework, open source investigators must understand the key concepts of cybersecurity and risk management. They must also be able to identify assets that need protecting and potential harms, and assess potential threats, risks and vulnerabilities.

70. Risk is the potential for loss, damage or destruction of an asset as a result of a threat exploiting a vulnerability. Each of these terms is defined below. Since open source investigations conducted on the Internet involve different methods of information-gathering to traditional investigations, they give rise to different types of risks. The identification and assessment of these risks is an essential part of the planning and preparation of an investigation. Some examples of common risks in open source investigations include: the technological capabilities and awareness of the target of an investigation, or entities supporting the target, who could evade or mislead the investigation; problems in the technical configuration of the online environment being used for the investigation that could lead to the exposure of information that could compromise the

investigation; malicious software or code that might compromise an investigator's computer systems, activities, identity or collected data; or technical features, such as trackers, cookies, beacons and analytics, that could compromise investigative activities.

71. The following section contains explanations of the key terms and their application to open source investigations, thus providing a road map for conducting a threat and risk assessment.

1. Assets

72. An asset is anything that needs to be protected, including people,[103] property and information. In the context of open source investigations, persons requiring protection may include investigators or investigation teams, including anyone with whom the investigators or investigation teams work (i.e. internal colleagues and external partners, both local and those working in the field), authors or sources of information, witnesses, victims, alleged perpetrators and bystanders. Property consists of tangible and intangible items that can be assigned a value.[104] Tangible assets include buildings, equipment and documents, whereas intangible assets include reputation and proprietary information, such as digital data, metadata, databases, software code and records.

2. Harm

73. Harm is physical or mental damage or injury to assets or the destruction thereof. It may involve digital, financial, legal, physical, psychosocial or reputational harm.

(a) Digital harm

74. Digital harm refers to damage to any digital information or infrastructure. Potential digital harm may include the destruction, manipulation or loss of access to data, or the disruption of services from computer systems and platforms.

---

[102] In addition to minimizing the risk of confusing the investigations, such practices will help effectively to preserve a chain of custody.

[103] Referring to people as assets is done only in the context of conducting security assessments.

[104] See Threat Analysis Group, "Threat, vulnerability, risk – commonly mixed up terms". Available at www.threatanalysis.com/2010/05/03/threat-vulnerability-risk-commonly-mixed-up-terms.

IV. SECURITY

(b)   Financial harm

75. Financial harm can arise from a number of sources, including the legal and reputational harm tied to an investigation. Investigators, targets and bystanders may all experience such harm. Additionally, financial harm may result when investigators fail to adequately assess the long-term costs of an investigation.

(c)   Legal harm

76. Open source investigators may accrue legal liability for either the process or outputs of their work. Investigators should be aware of the legal limitations on what they are permitted to do and the legal ramifications of their actions, in order to minimize the risk of legal liability for themselves and/ or third parties. Investigations can also result in legal harm for the subjects of such investigations, and even for bystanders, who may be implicated in legal wrongs that are uncovered during the course of an investigation.[105]

(d)   Physical harm

77. Physical harm may include damage to persons or property. While open source investigators usually work from an office or home, as opposed to being out in the field, physical harm should nevertheless be assessed as a potential consequence of online activities. Actions in cyberspace can lead to real-world consequences, of which investigators should be aware and for which they should be prepared. For example, open source investigators should be conscious of those individuals – whether colleagues, online users in situation countries or others – who may be in insecure environments and at risk of physical harm as a result of an investigator's online behaviour. Online investigators have an ethical – and in some cases legal – duty of care[106] to others to ensure that those who are at risk of physical harm are not placed in greater danger due to their activities. Physical risks should be considered as part of a comprehensive threat assessment prior to commencing work and re-evaluated throughout the life cycle of an investigation.

(e)   Psychosocial harm

78. Psychosocial harm can range from psychological distress to trauma, and can affect any member of an investigation team and/or persons otherwise involved in or affected by an investigation, including the subjects of an investigation and bystanders. In addition to the moral and ethical importance of protecting oneself and others from psychological harm, humans can sometimes be the most vulnerable link in any organization's effective functioning. A human suffering psychosocial harm may be especially vulnerable, creating new openings for threat actors to exploit or other risks to physical and digital security, especially if negative psychological effects result in compromised functioning, such as laxer-than-usual adherence to security protocols. Viewing large quantities of violent and otherwise graphic videos is known to be especially difficult to process, and can result in psychological distress or trauma, which may require professional support. Signs of secondary trauma may include changes in behaviour, mood swings, shifts in eating or drinking habits, an inability to sleep, a desire to sleep more than usual or nightmares.[107] Strategies for mitigating psychosocial harm are described in the section on preparing and creating a resilience plan and self-care.[108]

---

[105] See also chaps. IV.E and IV.F above for further discussion of the relevant legal considerations.

[106] Rome Statute, art. 54 (1) (b).

[107] See Dart Center for Journalism and Trauma, "Working with traumatic imagery", 12 August 2014 (available at https://dartcenter. org/content/working-with-traumatic-imagery); Sam Dubberley, Elizabeth Griffin and Haluk Mert Bal, *Making Secondary Trauma a Primary Issue: A Study of Eyewitness Media and Vicarious Trauma on the Digital Frontline* (Eyewitness Media Hub, 2015) (available at http://eyewitnessmediahub.com/research/vicarious-trauma); Sam Dubberley and Michele Grant, "Journalism and vicarious trauma: a guide for journalists, editors and news organisations" (First Draft News, 2017) (available at https://firstdraftnews.org/wp-content/ uploads/2017/04/vicarioustrauma.pdf); Center for Human Rights and Global Justice, "Human rights resilience project launches new website", 21 May 2018 (available at https://chrgj.org/2018/05/21/human-rights-resilience-project-launches-resources-for-resilience-website); Keramet Reiter and Alexa Koenig, "Reiter and Koenig on challenges and strategies for researching trauma", Palgrave MacMillan (available at www.palgrave.com/gp/blogs/social-sciences/reiter-and-koenig-on-researching-trauma).

[108] See chap. V.D below for further information on self-care.

(f) Reputational harm

79. Reputational harm, in the context of open source investigations, can be most acute for open source investigators and/or their organizations, for example, if investigators publish erroneous information, violate ethics or otherwise produce problematic content. Reputational harm may also accrue to the subjects of investigations, who may face stigma for their alleged behaviour once that behaviour is made public. This can be particularly concerning when accusations are made against persons or organizations that later turn out to be false.

3. Protection measures

80. Protection measures are efforts taken to prevent or minimize vulnerabilities and may include physical, technological and policy measures. Physical protection may include locks on buildings, rooms or cabinets in which sensitive material is stored. Technological measures may include the use of passwords, encryption and multifactor authentication on devices, or access controls on data systems. Policy measures include internal and external rules, laws and enforcement mechanisms, such as rules against sending internal work product from a work email to a personal email or policies against using personal social media accounts on one's work computer.

4. Threats

81. Threats are something that assets need to be protected against. A threat is anything that can exploit a vulnerability, intentionally or accidentally, and obtain, damage or destroy an asset. Threats can be internal or external to an organization or investigation and can be executed by individuals, groups, institutions or networks. Open sources investigators should be aware of the following threats, among others.

(a) Distributed denial-of-service attacks

82. Distributed denial-of-service attacks are cyberattacks designed to disrupt the ability of the target to access a machine or network. A system for mitigating such attacks should be put in place for public-facing assets, such as websites and other remote access portals. In addition, a system to log incidents should be put in place and used in the event of an attack to record all actions and the relevant actors.

(b) Phishing attacks

83. Phishing is the fraudulent attempt to obtain sensitive information, such as usernames, passwords and credit card details, by disguising oneself as a trustworthy entity in an electronic communication.[109] Phishing or telephone scams are used to gain confidential information or to harass investigators. Personal accounts are generally at higher risk than professional ones; thus, their use can jeopardize investigations or work product.

(c) Man-in-the-middle attacks

84. Man-in-the-middle attacks are a type of cyberattack in which malicious actors insert themselves into conversations between two parties, impersonate both parties and gain access to information that the two parties were trying to send to each other.[110] A man-in-the-middle attack allows a malicious actor to intercept, send and receive data meant for someone else, or not meant to be sent at all, without either outside party knowing until it is too late.[111]

(d) Social engineering

85. Social engineering is the psychological manipulation of people to get them to perform a potentially harmful action, such as revealing confidential information. There are many different examples of social engineering, such as spear phishing.[112] Since social engineering tactics continue to adapt and evolve, investigators should engage in ongoing training on the detection and avoidance of identified social engineering tactics.

---

[109] See Phishing.org, "What is phishing?". Available at www.phishing.org/what-is-phishing.

[110] See Veracode, "Man in the middle (MITM) attack". Available at www.veracode.com/security/man-middle-attack.

[111] Ibid.

[112] Spear phishing is the fraudulent practice of sending emails ostensibly from a known or trusted sender in order to induce targeted individuals to reveal confidential information.

(e) Malware

86.   Malware, short for malicious software, refers to computer programs designed to infiltrate and damage computers without the user's consent. There are several types of malware, including spyware and ransomware.

5.   Threat actors

87.   A threat actor or malicious actor is a person or entity that is responsible for an event or incident that has an impact, or has the potential to have an impact, on the safety or security of another entity or actor. In international criminal and human rights investigations, threat actors are likely to be the alleged perpetrators, the targets of an investigation, including Governments, or their supporters. It is important for open source investigators to identity potential threat actors and understand their capabilities and the likelihood of their launching attacks.

6.   Vulnerabilities

88.   A vulnerability is a weakness or gap in protection measures, which can exist in both the digital and physical realms. When it comes to online activities, vulnerabilities could include a weakness in security protection measures that could be exploited to gain unauthorized access to an asset, security defects in software, insecure design, and overprivileged users and code. Offline, they may also include weaknesses in people, such as a team member who is susceptible to blackmail or coercion, or who may become vulnerable as a result of overexposure to graphic material or as a result of other difficult working conditions.[113] New vulnerabilities may be created by exposing that an investigation is under way to the target or revealing the scope of an investigation. Finally, security vulnerabilities may come from external threats, such as new malware and viruses, of which investigators should be aware. A security mapping and risk assessment should take these kinds of vulnerabilities into account.

89.   Open source investigators should also be aware of the following online vulnerabilities.

(a) Cookies

90.   A cookie is a small file that is often sent through a website and stored either in a user's computer memory or written to a computer's disk, for use by a browser. Cookies are often necessary for a website to function correctly – for example, by offering the ability for users' website preferences and identity details to be stored in order to remove the need for them to repeatedly enter data during subsequent visits. Cookies have been developed so that they can gather and store significant – often sensitive – data about visitors and their visits. Some have evolved into centralized tools that can be used to collect data to help build a picture of a user's browsing interests and habits. A cookie may be present on a computer until such time as it expires or is deleted by a user.

(b) Trackers

91.   A tracker is a type of cookie that exploits the ability of a browser to keep a record of which web pages have been visited, which search criteria have been entered etc. Trackers are persistent cookies that keep a running log of a website visitor's behaviour. In their simplest form, trackers assign a unique identity to a user's browser and then link that identity to all subsequent browsing and search activity (search criteria, pages visited, sequence of pages visited etc.) This affords the owner of a tracker the ability to link previous and subsequent visits to a website (or set of affiliated websites) together to build a detailed picture of users and their browsing habits. Trackers are often built into advertisements, which are then distributed across multiple websites, offering the tracker a far greater chance of capturing user activity and behaviour. Even visiting a "trusted" website might result in trackers being installed on users' computers and their subsequent activities on the Internet being tracked.

---

[113]   See chap. V.D below for further information on resilience and self-care.

(c) Beacons

92. A beacon is a mechanism to track user activity and behaviour. Beacons are made from a small and unobtrusive (often invisible) element in a web page (something as small as a single transparent pixel) that, when rendered by a browser, results in details about that browser and affiliated computer being sent back to a third party. Beacons can be used alongside cookies to trigger data collection and transmission and to uniquely identify users and record their browsing habits. Beacons are closely related with social media sites, where the identification of relationships and networks are the key building-blocks for the sites. Finally, beacons can be used within HTML-based email to collect and report on user identity and to access any cookies that were previously stored on that computer.

(d) Other codes and scripts

93. An increasing number of websites are making use of small pieces of code that are downloaded by a visitor's browser, which have the ability to store information about the visit. Such code can influence how the website appears, how the website reacts to inputs and how a browser responds to the website. Code can also store sensitive data related to visitors' credentials, activities etc. Data collection may be persistent and may send data to a third party.

C. Infrastructure-related considerations

94. Infrastructure refers to the structures, facilities and systems, including both software and hardware, needed to conduct open source investigations. The infrastructure should provide (and be provided with) sufficient security measures to protect and preserve an organization's assets and data. For infrastructure resilience, mitigation measures should be in place to ensure continuity in the event of any of the following:

(a) Disruption or loss of an Internet connection;

(b) Disruption or loss of access to stored data;

(c) Loss, corruption or destruction of data;

(d) Disruption or loss of software services;

(e) Damage to or loss of hardware;

(f) Unauthorized access to devices;

(g) Unauthorized access to a network;

(h) Accidental deletion or manipulation of data;

(i) Intentional destruction or manipulation of data;

(j) Leakage of data or data being held "hostage".

95. The necessary architecture is defined by the scale of the online investigative activities to be performed, the nature of the investigation and the subject of interest, as well as the finances available to build, sustain and modify the infrastructure as needed.

1. Infrastructure

96. The infrastructure used for open source investigations will include the following components at a minimum, with additional features relevant to specific investigative strategies.

(a) Devices

97. Open source investigators must have equipment for accessing online content, such as a desktop computer, laptop, tablet or smartphone. Hardware and equipment should be password protected, have full-disk encryption enabled and ideally use multifactor authentication.[114] All equipment should be regularly backed up. When not in use, hardware should be stored securely with access restricted to the user and approved personnel. Personal equipment should not be used for work-related activities. Similarly, investigation-related equipment should not be used for personal activities due to the risk of linking personal social media to

---

[114] Multifactor authentication is a security enhancement that requires a user to present two types of credentials to log in to an account, e.g. providing both a password and a biometric (fingerprint) or smart card. See United States, National Institute of Standards and Technology, "Back to basics: multi-factor authentication (MFA)". Available at www.nist.gov/itl/applied-cybersecurity/tig/back-basics-multi-factor-authentication.

virtual identities cultivated for the purpose of an investigation.[115]

(b) Internet connection

98. Ideally, investigators will have a strong, stable and private Internet connection and should avoid using public Wi-Fi. While free, public Wi-Fi – including semi-private networks, such as those provided by hotels or Internet cafes – offers a convenient option, it is very insecure and susceptible to numerous threats, the biggest of which is the ability of hackers to position themselves between a user and the connection point. Using a personal, password-protected hotspot does require financial investment, but it is essential for conducting secure online investigative activities. In addition, while not always under an investigator's control, a strong and stable Internet connection is preferable as regards both functionality and security. If using a virtual private network (VPN) on an unstable connection, investigators should put in place a fail-safe mechanism to ensure that, if the connection drops, their IP address is not exposed.

(c) Web browsers

99. One of the core tools used in online investigations is a web browser, which is used to query, search for and access websites published on the Internet. Browsers act as the primary interface between investigators and the Internet yet are often overlooked as a source of risk. Modern browsers are continuously being modified and have a wide range of built-in functionalities to accommodate a multitude of requirements. Browsers are also a key target for those wishing to conduct surveillance or to launch attacks against an adversary, as functionality can be misused and additional functionality can be added with relative ease. A browser has simultaneous access to the Internet and to the computer and, correspondingly, potentially identifying information about the user. Data leakage through a browser may disclose sufficient data to alert the subject

of an investigation. Modern browsers have several built-in features and can have multiple additional features added, known as browser add-ons, which may individually or collectively leak data, leading to identification of an investigation, an investigator or a line of inquiry and associated search activities. Browsers are also, by default, able to download and execute computer code derived from a website. The presence and/or function of the computer code may not be apparent to investigators, yet the code may be able to alter the digital content delivered to them, access functionality and data on their computers and even cause computers to behave in a different manner from that envisaged. Open source investigators should seek to minimize these risks by ensuring that they use secure, updated browsers that are regularly screened and by using appropriate software and plug-ins installed that mitigate against some of the risks described above.[116]

2. Security measures

100. These essential elements of infrastructure can be used to identify users and their locations. In order to comply with the principle of anonymity and non-attribution, investigators should employ the following strategies to camouflage their Internet connections. Such strategies mask the location and IP address and camouflage the machine, masking its identifying features, operating system and browser.

(a) Connection camouflage

101. An IP address can give away information that could be used to target an organization's infrastructure. Open source investigators should seek to use VPNs, proxies or other software to mask their computers' IP addresses, meaning that the IP addresses disclosed to the Internet are not linked to the investigators or their organizations. VPNs also create an encrypted channel for communications between an investigator's computer and the VPN server, such that any networks/nodes that the connection passes though would only see encrypted data,

---

[115] This recommendation may be difficult to comply with during travel, as many investigators will bring their work device but want or need to conduct personal business out of hours. Therefore, organizations conducting open source investigations should develop reasonable travel policies.

[116] For up-to-date guidance on browsers and other operational security measures, see the Computer Security Resource Center of the United States National Institute of Standards and Technology (https://csrc.nist.gov).

which provides an additional layer of protection. However, the use of certain VPNs is blocked by some countries and websites, and can flag investigative activities as potentially suspect to third parties. Ideally, VPNs should allow investigators to use multiple IP addresses with the ability to rapidly switch between them when necessary. IP addresses should not be traceable to a single country, but split so that they reflect multiple locations across the world.

(b) Machine camouflage

102. In order to mask certain features that could be used to identify users, investigators can use virtual machines, which are software programs or operating systems that exhibit the behaviour of distinct computers. The use of a virtual machine will essentially create a new computer within a computer – a completely separate environment from the rest of a computer. A virtual machine is also capable of performing tasks such as running applications and programs as if it were a separate computer altogether,[117] making the investigator who uses it appear as a different subject online. When using a virtual machine, investigators have a system to vary the browser, user agent, software, opened ports, operating system and other information about the machine in order to appear as a different subject each time they go online. Ideally, the infrastructure would allow an investigator to use a virtual machine that masks the actual machine being used. Virtual machines may be destroyed and recreated, restored to a previous point, configured in different ways, replicated for new cases or preserved for future needs. Alternatively, investigators can take the more burdensome but also relatively effective approach of varying their appearance manually, by using different browsers each time they go online, changing settings to limit the uniqueness of their machines' fingerprints, and using plug-ins that prevent tracking.

3. Other infrastructure

103. Before beginning their work, investigators should consider other infrastructure to protect their networks and infrastructure, including the following systems:

(a) Backup systems;

(b) Log systems to audit activities and track user actions;

(c) Segregated storage systems and suitable storage locations to collect digital materials identified during searches. In order to protect data from the outside, organizations should have platforms (such as evidence repositories, databases or other information management systems) that are kept separate from the primary networks. Platforms should have two main parts: one connected to the Internet and the other disconnected. In some instances, it may be appropriate to remove data from the Internet-connected infrastructure to a more secure network/repository as soon as possible, so that the information can be reviewed safely.

D. User-related considerations

104. One of the weakest points in any security framework is the user. Even with perfect infrastructure in place, security principles will not be adhered to without adapting user behaviour through regular training and oversight. Security is everyone's responsibility. Individuals should not engage in activities that could put data or persons at risk without proper training on how to mitigate those risks. Investigators should be trained to assess which behaviour is appropriate when conducting different online activities.

105. Anonymity can help minimize harm in situations in which a threat actor attempts a trace back of the origin of activity to the network or user.[118] Any online activity is vulnerable to being tracked by third parties; therefore, investigators should assume such a threat when conducting online activities. The most common objects of a trace include IP addresses, browsers and screen resolution (used to identify equipment), as well as navigation time and activity on websites (such

---

[117] See Techopedia, "Virtual machine (VM)", 21 May 2020. Available at www.techopedia.com/definition/4805/virtual-machine-vm.

[118] To trace back is to discover the point of origin of someone or something by following a trail of information or series of events backwards.

as the search terms entered or pages visited). A threat actor may attempt to identify the source of online activity. If a trace back is attempted, a threat actor should be directed away from the true location or identity of an investigator or investigating entity. This can be done by taking measures to appear to the Internet as if access is from somewhere else, through the use of a VPN, for example, or as someone else, through the creation and use of virtual identities.[119]

106. Masking the connection and the machine being used in an online investigation provides important protection, but such protection may be undermined if users reveal themselves by self-identifying on a website or, for example, by using personal information to register or log in to a social media platform or other private account. Investigators should never use their personal accounts to investigate or log in to personal accounts in a browser used for open source investigations. Some accounts may require the use of photographs, telephone numbers or emails at the time of creation. Photographs, telephones, emails or data that are personal or attributable to investigators or others should never be used.

User camouflage

107. A virtual identity[120] is a false online identity or profile that can be used to conduct secure investigative activities on social media platforms and other open web-based platforms that require users to log in to access content. This can also include a virtual account or an email or messaging service, database, product or application that uses a false online identity rather than one's real life identity. Open source investigators should, from a security perspective, create and use virtual identities for online investigative activities of open source material. This is in order to ensure that if a threat actor attempts to trace the online activities of that profile, they will find consistent and convincing information based on the virtual identity that does not reveal real information about an investigator or an investigating entity, or information about the content or focus of an investigation. This is also an important security measure to protect those who may be supporting an investigation. Virtual profiles and accounts and activities conducted with their use should be planned,[121] records should be maintained of the information used to create the accounts and activities using such accounts should be recorded so that they can be explained later if needed, for example, in court.[122]

---

[119] For a discussion of virtual identities, see also chap. II.C, chap. III.F, and chap. IV.A and C above.

[120] Any use of virtual identities should balance the need for security with the ethical principle of transparency. See chap. II.C above on ethical principles.

[121] See chap. V.C below on the online investigation plan.

[122] See chap. VI.D below on preservation.

PREPARATION

CHAPTER SUMMARY

- Preparation and strategic planning are key to a thorough and secure investigation.

- Preparation includes three processes: (a) assessing threats and risks and devising a plan for mitigating those threats and risks; (b) assessing the information landscape; and (c) developing an investigation plan. These processes may overlap and/or repeat throughout the investigation life cycle.

- Preparation includes developing a plan to handle any negative psychosocial aspects of an investigation, such as that which may result from exposure to graphic or otherwise potentially traumatic material.

- Preparation includes developing a plan for how to handle any information collected throughout its life cycle, including when and under which conditions it should be deleted, how and under which conditions it can be shared and who should have access.

- Preparation should include an assessment of potentially useful software and other tools. Investigators should understand the trade-offs between commercial, custom-built and open source resources.

108. Open source investigators should only begin online investigative activities after certain preparatory measures have been taken. Preparatory steps should include conducting a digital threat and risk assessment and a digital landscape assessment.[123] Investigators should then develop online investigation plans, integrating insights from those assessments. Each of these activities is detailed below.

109. At an organizational level, it is also important to establish policies on data retention, data deletion, data access and data-sharing before information is collected and preserved, as detailed below.

A. Digital threat and risk assessment

110. Thinking about potential threats and adopting a strategy to manage risk – whether physical, digital or psychosocial – will ensure compliance with security and ethical principles. At the outset, a digital threat and risk assessment should be conducted, identifying general and case-specific threats that may arise as a result of online activities, particularly visiting target websites, conducting ongoing monitoring of specific sources or scraping of data from social media platforms. The assessment should involve elements of traditional threat analysis, such as identifying all potential threat actors, assessing the interests and capabilities of those threat actors, and the probability of attack, considering vulnerabilities and putting protection measures in place to minimize those vulnerabilities. Such an assessment will benefit from consultations with, or input from, security experts, particularly those with cybersecurity expertise.[124] The assessment should be periodically reviewed and updated as

necessary. In addition, further assessments may be needed to address specific types of online activities or the introduction of new potential threat actors.[125]

B. Digital landscape assessment

111. Open source investigators should understand the digital environment of the situation under investigation. The type of technology available and used, including by whom, will have an impact on the types of digital data available. This requires identifying the most commonly used online platforms, communications services, social media platforms, mobile technologies and mobile applications used in the geographic region under investigation. For example, in war crimes investigations, investigators will need to know the types of transportation, ITC and digital media used by all parties involved in the armed conflict, as well as that of bystanders or other witnesses, in order to know which types of information are most likely to be captured and distributed online.

112. Investigators should examine the categories of people who use or have access to each of those technologies within that geographic region. In this regard, investigators should be aware that user-generated publicly available digital content, including social media posts and information shared through networking platforms, may not equally capture the full scope of violations against all individuals and groups. This is because the use of digital technologies may be different based on, inter alia, gender,[126] ethnicity, religion, belief, age, socioeconomic status, membership of a racial, linguistic,[127] ethnic or religious minority, indigenous identity, migration status and

---

[123] See below, annex II on the digital threat and risk assessment template and annex III on the digital landscape assessment template.

[124] For general information on threats and risk in open source investigations, see chap. IV above on security.

[125] See annex II below on the digital threat and risk assessment template.

[126] E.g., women, girls and lesbian, gay, bisexual, transgender and intersex persons may not have access to, or be the holders of, the family mobile telephone. For further discussion on what has been termed the "gender digital divide", see A/HRC/35/9. See also Human Rights Council resolution 32/13, and Araba Sey and Nancy Hafkin, eds., *Taking Stock: Data and Evidence on Gender Equality in Digital Access, Skills, and Leadership* (Macao, China, EQUALS Global Partnership and the United Nations University, 2019). Available at www.itu.int/en/action/gender-equality/Documents/EQUALS%20Research%20Report%202019.pdf.

[127] Those belonging to linguistic minorities, e.g., may face barriers in terms of accessing online space, which is usually run in the dominant language. However, some linguistic minorities may also have their own online space run by or using their own languages. Therefore, investigators may need to search through minority languages (including in indigenous languages).

geographic location.[128] This imbalance may be a result of lack of access to devices, facilities or resources,[129] whereby those individuals do not have the opportunity to create or upload online information about issues or violations concerning them. Another factor may be that those mentioned, among others, may not have had access to equal education and therefore have less capacity in terms of technical skills. As a result of intersecting forms of discrimination, certain segments of society might be doubly invisible online. For example, information on women and girls belonging to one of the aforementioned marginalized groups may be even less represented in open source information. These factors can mean that such persons are not the ones creating content, or being captured by the content, thereby skewing the results of any online investigation.

113. Furthermore, the unequal access to technology by all segments of society may also skew not only the focus on who is represented in online content, but also the types of violations that are available online, in particular with regard to user-generated content. For example, when women share the use of mobile telephones owned by their male family members, or share an account with others, they may not discuss sensitive issues, such as sexual and gender-based violence, or issues around sexual and reproductive health. Moreover, user-generated content on social media, including photographs and videos, might more easily depict certain violations than others. For example, sexual and gender-based violence, which might be perpetrated in private settings, may be harder to depict than photographs of evictions, for example.

114. While some of these factors can be mitigated by seeking to access a plurality of types of online information, not just user-generated content, the same factors must be considered when analysing other types of open source

information. For example, when accessing government-generated data and statistics, investigators should always question whether data have accurately captured all segments and aspects of society.[130] There are a number of key issues and technologies that can be assessed, depending on what is relevant to a specific investigation based on its geographic and temporal scope. Investigators should take into consideration gender, age, geography, socioeconomic disparities and other relevant demographic information. The goal of this assessment is to improve investigators' understanding of the situations under investigation in order to design effective online investigative strategies, as well as to force investigators to consider upfront potential biases in the data available online. All of these categories may not be relevant to all investigations, so investigators should adapt the digital landscape assessment to what is appropriate to their specific case.[131] For a complete list of categories of information that can be included in a digital landscape assessment, see annex III below.

C. Online investigation plan

115. Before beginning an open source investigation, an online investigation plan[132] should be created that covers (a) the overall investigative strategy; and (b) specific online investigative activities. If online investigations are part of a broader investigation using traditional techniques, such as taking witnesses' statements or gathering physical evidence, the online investigation plan should be integrated into the main investigation plan. Investigators should integrate a gender perspective into the investigation plan to ensure that the investigation extends to all gender-relevant concerns and takes into account the differentiated nature of access to technology.[133] An online investigation plan should address the following topics.

---

[128] E.g., in rural areas, connectivity to the Internet may be less.

[129] Such as not having physical access to a fast Internet connection or not being able to afford devices or pay subscription fees.

[130] See, generally, OHCHR, "A human rights-based approach to data: leaving no one behind in the 2030 Agenda for Sustainable Development" (Geneva, 2018). Available at www.ohchr.org/Documents/Issues/HRIndicators/GuidanceNoteonApproachtoData.pdf.

[131] For the template, see annex III below.

[132] See annex I below on the online investigation plan template.

[133] For further guidance on how to integrate a gender perspective, see *Integrating a Gender Perspective into Human Rights Investigations: Guidance and Practice* (United Nations publication, Sales No. 19.XIV.2).

1. Objectives and planned activities

116. The plan should specify the objectives and priorities of the open source investigation, the proposed strategy for meeting these objectives and a timeline for their implementation.

2. Risk management strategy

117. The plan should include key findings of the above-mentioned digital threat and risk assessment, such as potential cyberthreats, along with a strategy for managing risk, including how to identify, respond to and recover from breaches or attacks.

3. Mapping actors and cooperation opportunities

118. Open source investigators may want to map the other actors who are conducting similar or overlapping investigations to assess how their activities might affect each other and to explore potential partnerships and opportunities for collaboration. This may include identifying digital archivists, journalists or other groups or individuals who are preserving online content that might be relevant to an investigation. This mapping should also take into account potential bias and the limitations of other actors, which may result in findings by third parties that do not fully capture the complexities of a given situation, or may exclude certain groups due to the inherent bias of the digital sphere that is not accommodated for, as described above. If such partnerships are formed, it can be helpful to establish a written agreement for information-sharing.

4. Resources

119. The plan should identify the resources needed to conduct the planned activities, including staffing, training, tools and equipment. An assessment of staffing needs may include the number of team members needed to carry out tasks, their competencies, the inclusivity and diversity of the team members

and an evaluation of additional training requirements. This may include an assessment of the infrastructure that is necessary, including hardware and software, and the financial costs of preserving digital material in the long term. The plan should also ensure that there are dedicated resources for the gender-sensitive psychological well-being of investigators, particularly in situations in which an open source investigation is dealing with graphic content or investigators or implicated third parties may be particularly at risk of reprisals if their identities or privacy are compromised.[134]

5. Roles and responsibilities

120. If working in a team or with external partners, the roles and responsibilities of open source investigators should be well defined, taking into consideration the need to coordinate activities, including the need to avoid duplicating activities and data collection. In addition, this section of the plan should consider which specialized areas of expertise might be needed for the specific investigation and whether the investigators will need to consult or engage an expert if there is not one in the existing team. Specialized areas of expertise may include digital forensics, satellite imagery analysis and data science. In certain areas of expertise, proactive efforts may be needed to identify experts from diverse gender and other backgrounds in order to ensure the inclusivity and diversity of the investigation team and its analysis.

6. Documentation

121. Open source investigations should be documented in a manner that allows for their efficient management and compliance with the principle of accountability. In the event of legal proceedings, this documentation should enable investigators to demonstrate that the evidence collected is relevant and probative and to explain the steps taken, or not taken, during the course of online activities and why. Whether self-tasking or tasked by a supervisor, the

---

134 E.g., investigators may face online hate speech or harassment and those attacks may be gendered (e.g. women and lesbian, gay, bisexual, transgender, queer and intersex investigators may face higher than average risks of online hate speech, doxing, rape threats and other violent threats of a sexual or gender-based nature). See, e.g., Amnesty International, "Toxic Twitter – a toxic place for women". Available at www.amnesty.org/en/latest/research/2018/03/online-violence-against-women-chapter-1/.

system should have a mechanism for creating tasks for specific investigative activities, including online activities, such as requests to research a specific person or other queries. Task results, including reports, should reference the methodologies and techniques used. Reporting should separate operational information that may need to be kept confidential to protect an investigation's sources and methods from investigative information that must be disclosed during legal proceedings.

122. The online investigation plan should be reviewed on a regular basis and amended as necessary. See annex I below for the online investigation plan template.

D. Resilience plan and self-care

123. While open source investigators may not conduct in-person interviews or physically visit crime scenes, the particularities of digital research means that they may be exposed to viewing, collecting and analysing significant quantities of graphic or otherwise traumatic digital information, which can lead to secondary trauma, among other issues. Open source investigators should be aware of the principles of self-care,[135] and investigation managers should develop an organizational environment that values self-care and gender and cultural sensitivity. This should be instituted at the preparatory stage of an investigation, through the development of a plan to foster resilience and mitigate the negative psychosocial impacts of the investigation, which may have different effects depending on gender, culture and age. Such a plan is essential for ethical reasons, as part of the promotion and respect for the human rights of each member of an investigation team. It is also essential in order to maximize physical and digital security. Even with proper training, a stressed individual can represent a vulnerability for the safety of a team, the security of information and the quality of the work. Dedicated time and resources should be allocated to ensure the proper execution of the plan, in particular when it is anticipated that an online investigation may involve viewing large quantities of graphic images, including violent or otherwise disturbing content. Strategies for mitigating the potential negative impact of viewing graphic content are diverse but tend to fall into three categories: individual awareness, tactics for minimizing exposure and community support.

124. First, investigators should have an awareness of their own and their teammates' baseline behaviours, including patterns of work, recreation, sleeping and eating, so that deviations can be detected and addressed. Having a policy of investigators working in pairs can help with detection, since individuals may not recognize or want to acknowledge their own changes in behaviour, which may be more easily noted by others. Team members should be sensitive to and respectful of differences in responses to graphic and other material that may elicit strong emotion, and recognize that such differences may vary among individuals, genders and cultural groups, as well as over time for specific individuals due to the degree of stress they are under and other situational factors. Investigators should also recognize that having an emotional response to graphic or egregious content is often quite normal and is not a sign of weakness, but can be a sign of healthy functioning – and even strength.

125. Second, tactics should be adopted for minimizing exposure to harmful content. Common strategies in this regard include turning off the audio when viewing potentially graphic content for the first time or when not necessary for the immediate analytical task, since so much emotive content is embedded in sound; minimizing the size of screens to the extent possible; covering graphic material when analysing the context around a particular act and not the act itself; flagging any graphic content contained in a data set so that individuals do not view that content without previously knowing what they are about to see; warning each other when sharing graphic content in order to mitigate the element of surprise; working in pairs; avoiding working in isolation or late at night; and taking regular breaks, as needed.

---

[135] For further discussion of the importance of self-care for those working in the field of human rights investigations, see OHCHR, *Manual on Human Rights Monitoring* (Geneva, 2011), chap. 12 on trauma and self-care, pp. 20–39. Available at www.ohchr.org/Documents/ Publications/Chapter12-MHRM.pdf.

126. Third, individuals and organizations should foster a sense of community among team members, which can have a protective effect – essentially reproducing the sense of comradery that can occur when conducting investigations in the field. This can be achieved through regular debriefings, which can reduce isolation and help investigators better understand the positive impacts of their work; team outings, including celebrations of important investigatory milestones; and team training on resilience strategies. Attempts to increase resiliency can be especially impactful when addressed at the individual, cultural and structural levels, for example by empowering individuals to think critically about their psychosocial needs when working on an investigation and fostering an environment in which the psychosocial aspects of the work are taken seriously, supportive practices are both explicitly and implicitly encouraged and inclusivity and diversity are embraced.

E. Data policies and tools

127. Policies regarding the handling, preservation and destruction of data should be developed, implemented and complied with in the course of an investigation. Organizations should develop policies to preserve information (retention policies) and delete information (deletion policies), when appropriate, as well as policies regarding access to information (internally) and information-sharing (externally). Additionally, specific policies on the creation and use of virtual identities, as well as access to approved software and the tools used may also be beneficial.

1. Data policies

(a) Data retention policies

128. Data retention policies are important in order to comply with many data protection laws and data retention regulations. In some cases, there are minimum requirements for how long data must be retained, while in other circumstances there is a maximum limit on how long data can

be retained. Policies should outline approaches to the storage of persistent data and records management with a view to meeting legal and business data archival requirements. Different data retention policies weigh legal and privacy concerns against economic and need-to-know concerns to determine retention times, archival rules, data formats and the permissible means of storage, access and encryption.[136] Understanding the rules that apply will be necessary for crafting such policies.

(b) Data deletion policies

129. Deleting portions of a data set without clear deletion and retention policies and without logs of what was deleted, by whom and when – and for what purposes – can raise significant problems, in particular when information may be used in court. Investigators should comply with applicable regulations regarding the deletion of digital data and be aware that there may be legal issues associated with using one method over another.

(c) Data access policies

130. Organizations collecting and processing data, particularly sensitive data, should have a clear policy of who can access various types of data. Any settings within databases or systems should be set to reflect this policy.

(d) Data-sharing policies

131. Organizations may want to consider crafting a policy for sharing data with external actors. If working with external partners, memorandums of understanding or contracts should be put in place to ensure that partners comply with such policies.

2. Information management

132. Before engaging in open source investigations, particularly in the collection and preservation of digital material, investigators, teams and organizations should establish an information management system. There are a range of options for such a system, and the Protocol

---

[136] Yvonne Ng, "How to preserve open source information effectively", in *Digital Witness, Using Open Source Information for Human Rights Investigation, Documentation and Accountability*, Sam Dubberley, Alexa Koenig and Daragh Murray, eds. (Oxford, Oxford University Press, 2020), pp. 143–164.

does not advocate for a specific one. Instead, the following provides the main functionalities that can be helpful for the investigation process – and, in some contexts, may be required. In addition, as discussed in chapter IV, infrastructure and protocols for security should be in place.

(a) Investigation management system

133. An investigation management system is a system for documenting activities conducted as part of an investigation. Not all organizations conducting investigations have such systems, but they are highly recommended, particularly for larger organizations or investigation teams. Such systems can be used to assign tasks and report on activities, so that the process is structured and as efficient as possible, as it can help reduce duplication of efforts.

(b) Information and evidence management systems

134. Information management systems are used to store the data collected as part of investigations. The information management system should be able to serve two distinct functions: (a) tracking the collection and handling of material; and (b) separating material that might be used as evidence.

3. Infrastructure – logistical and security considerations

135. Whether designing the infrastructure for an organization engaged in open source investigations or deciding which tools to use as an independent investigator, there are several important logistical and security considerations. Generally, there are three approaches to systems development: (a) custom-building systems and tools; (b) using open source or free tools and software available on the Internet; or (c) purchasing commercial products from third parties. Each of these approaches comes with benefits and drawbacks, and their success depends on the specific circumstances and context in which investigators are operating. Here again, the Protocol does not advocate for one approach over another, but presents the benefits and drawbacks of each, as well as specific factors that should be taken into consideration when making decisions about which products to use.

(a) Commercial products

136. The benefit of commercial products is that a private business may have better infrastructure for security and be able to provide ongoing and consistent technical support. However, commercial products bear the obvious downside of cost. In addition, interacting with and relying on third parties might be a problem for organizations trying to keep their investigations confidential. Many commercial products have closed-source code to protect their intellectual property. Commercial products may also raise concerns about data ownership, portability and exportability of data, and interoperability with other systems. Furthermore, companies may respond to government pressure for access to private information. A key concern is that, while companies have security teams to protect their products and users, those users have to trust that the companies have designed and will maintain their systems properly, and that there will be no hidden costs at a later stage.

(b) Custom-built or customized tools

137. The benefit of custom-building a tool from scratch or customizing a tool that already exists is that investigators or organizations maintain control over the entire system and their data and, as a result, can avoid interacting with third parties. Custom-built systems can also be easier to integrate with other bespoke systems. The downside is the time, cost and expertise required to build and support such systems, which will be a challenge for most organizations. In addition, a closed system with limited beta testers and users can make it difficult to identify vulnerabilities or obtain sufficient feedback to maximize functionality.

(c) Open source and free tools

138. Open source tools are tools for which the developers have openly published the source codes so that anyone can freely use or modify them. Some commercial products exist with open-source codes and some free tools are available with closed-source codes, but these are the exceptions. Most commonly, open source tools are free. For smaller organizations with restricted budgets, as well as larger organizations that have burdensome procurement procedures for paid products, free tools can be an important alternative to

consider. However, tools that are free for users may make a profit in other ways, such as selling user data and analytics, which raises security and privacy issues. In addition, use of these tools requires prior research in order to know who created them, whether they have been independently audited and if they are sustainable. All three aspects could undermine the credibility of an investigation. In particular, tools could be problematic in the legal context if a case goes to trial and a tool is challenged by the opposing party. Additionally, these software systems and tools require a backup plan, and a data migration and backup system, in case they become obsolete or the developers become unavailable. While open source tools may be attractive to organizations, in part due to the fact that other, like-minded groups are using them, investigators must conduct full, independent assessments of how they work and the implications that their use may have in a particular context.

139. When making a decision about whether to custom-build a tool, use free-trial or open-source software or purchase a product, investigators should follow the due diligence guidance provided in annex V below.

INVESTIGATION PROCESS

CHAPTER SUMMARY

- There are six main phases to the investigation process. These are (a) online inquiry; (b) preliminary assessment; (c) collection; (d) preservation; (e) verification; and (f) investigative analysis. Collectively, these are part of a cycle that may be repeated numerous times throughout the course of an investigation, as newly discovered information leads to new lines of inquiry.

- Investigators should document their activities during each phase. This will help with the understandability and transparency of their investigations, including chains of custody, and with the efficiency and efficacy of their investigations, including completeness and communication among team members.

140. Open source investigations require careful observation and systematic inquiries in order to establish facts in a complex and dynamic digital environment. Open source investigators must use a critical eye to vet online content and be able to assess the ways in which digital material can be distorted or manipulated. They should also apply a structured approach to querying the Internet, accounting for algorithmic bias and inequality regarding the availability of open source information pertaining to specific groups and the dynamic nature of online information. Every alleged fact should be rigorously examined. This chapter provides a structured approach to open source investigations. The figure below depicts the open source investigation cycle. It is important to note that open source investigations are rarely linear and often require repetition of this process given the cyclical nature of case-building. There may also be valid reasons for diverging from this order.

Open source investigation cycle

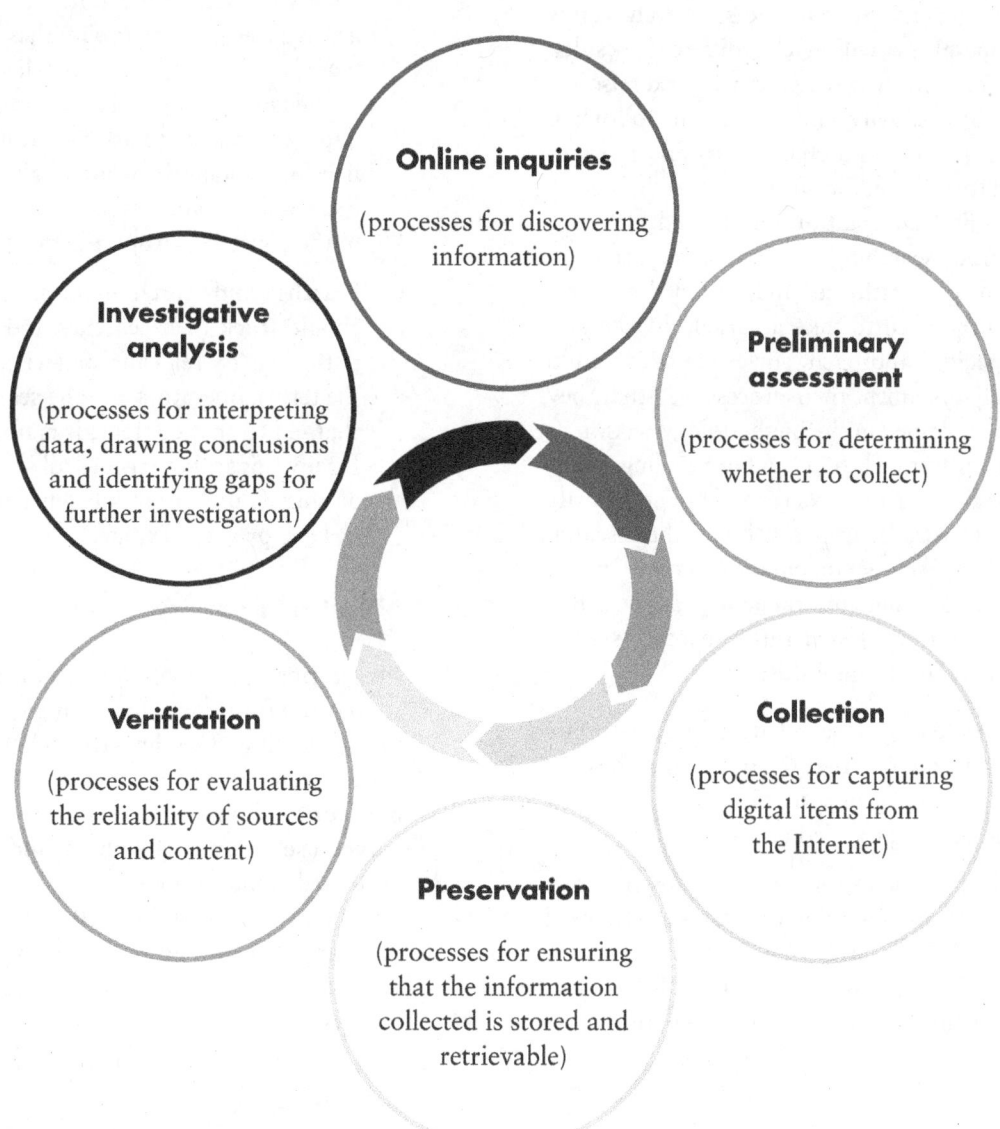

Online inquiries

(processes for discovering information)

Investigative analysis

(processes for interpreting data, drawing conclusions and identifying gaps for further investigation)

Preliminary assessment

(processes for determining whether to collect)

Verification

(processes for evaluating the reliability of sources and content)

Collection

(processes for capturing digital items from the Internet)

Preservation

(processes for ensuring that the information collected is stored and retrievable)

A. Online inquiries

141. There are two main processes for online inquiries: (a) searching, that is discovering information and information sources through the use of general or advanced search methodologies; and (b) monitoring, that is discovering new information through the consistent and persistent review of a set of constant sources.

1. Searching

142. Online searching is a task-oriented activity aimed at discovering new information relevant to a defined objective or research question. Searches should be structured and systematic, including beginning with a clear research question and search parameters, as well as keywords and operators.[137] Different search engines, search tools, search terms and operators will yield different results; therefore, investigators must exercise a degree of creativity and tenacity in following various avenues and channels to find relevant information. In addition to the search engines used to find information on indexed websites, structured searching can also be used on social media platforms and within databases. Due to the need to take a varied, diverse and case-specific approach, investigators should carefully document their processes so that they can be explained in the methodology section of reports or testified to in legal proceedings. This may be a retroactive process and not necessarily one that proceeds in parallel with the research itself. However, documentation should always be done as contemporaneously as possible. Documentation of structured searches should include the following information:

    (a) Objective and research questions: articulate the question(s) that the online search seeks to answer, keeping in mind the principle of objectivity provided above;

    (b) Facts, assumptions, and unknowns: start from a point at which the facts are known, if such facts have been established. It also might be useful to work from the basis of lead information or logical assumptions, even if they have not yet been verified. However, it is essential that any assumptions are recorded as such. Finally, it can be valuable to articulate the gaps in knowledge or other "unknowns" at the outset of an investigation. Delineating these categories of information will help prevent biased or skewed outcomes by clarifying the search terms and their bases;

    (c) Search terms and keywords: in order to conduct a targeted search, investigators should create keyword lists that comply with the principle of objectivity based on the theory or multiple theories of the case. Investigators will ideally use keywords in all relevant languages and scripts and will be cautious about the potential for over-inclusive or under-inclusive search results. Despite variations in cases, there are certain general topics that should be incorporated into keyword lists, such as significant locations, names, organizations, dates and relevant hashtags. It may also be helpful to identify what might qualify as incriminating and exonerating information in the context of a specific investigation;

    (d) Searches and search engines: investigators should track their searches and record the pathways to relevant material, including the terms, operators and the search engines that led to that content. It is not necessary for investigators to record all search results, as this would be unduly burdensome and of little probative value.

2. Monitoring

143. Monitoring involves following an established source of information, for example a particular topic, over time. The aim is to track the changing content generated by a constant source. Online monitoring should be a structured activity that makes use of lists of known and previously evaluated online sources, such as websites or social media accounts, as well as search queries that are run on an ongoing basis against defined targets. See, for example, the following sources:

---

[137] Boolean operators are simple words, such as "and", "or" and "not", which can be used "to combine or exclude keywords in a search, resulting in more focused and productive results". See Alliant International University Library, "What is a Boolean operator?" Available at https://library.alliant.edu/screens/boolean.pdf.

(a) Websites and social media accounts: investigators should maintain working lists of websites and profiles to be monitored, which should include a justification for why they are being monitored; the person in charge of monitoring; who does the monitoring; and the frequency of monitoring;

(b) Hashtags and keywords: investigators should also maintain and regularly update a working list of hashtags and keywords that are being monitored;

(c) Automation: monitoring may involve the use of automated tools, which may, for example, periodically conduct a search on specific sites or by using certain parameters. Use of such tools, including their names and versions, and the information entered into them should always be recorded.

3. Bias

144. When conducting structured search and monitoring activities, open source investigators must always remain vigilant of bias – both their own cognitive bias and the inherent bias in the information available online. For example, if an investigator is searching for information on rape, the majority of data provided, or issues discussed online, will likely be about rape against women of reproductive age committed outside of marital relations. Search results could underreport less visible or reported types of rape, such as sexual violence against men and boys, lesbian, gay, bisexual, transgender and intersex persons, and older women and instances of marital rape.

145. Another example is investigations of violence incited by online hate speech, since such speech often incorporates and depends on coded language and symbols that are not easily detected by human investigators or machines. Especially when investigators come from outside the communities targeted, they may be unaware of the cultural and context-specific use of the terms and symbols used to incite hatred or violence. This is complicated by the fact that online hate speech is often deliberately designed to avoid detection by machine or human monitors in order to avoid being removed from online platforms, while in fact being aimed at inciting violence or discrimination against a target population. In order to help overcome the difficulty of detecting incitement to discrimination, hostility or violence, investigators should apply a human rights-based test, as, for example, provided in the Rabat Plan of Action on the prohibition of advocacy of national, racial or religious hatred that constitutes incitement to discrimination, hostility or violence.[138]

146. Ultimately, the best way for investigators to counteract "bias in the machine" together with their bias is by being aware of the potential for such bias, recognizing risks and taking active steps when possible to counterbalance biases by researching the terminology and symbols that are relevant to a particular context or set of crimes or incidents, and broadening and diversifying the online inquiry. In cases involving sexual and gender-based violence, as well as any other crimes in which survivors are stigmatized and coded language is used, investigators should consult with experts who may be able to identify and share the coded language and communication practices that such survivors and perpetrators often use when communicating in online spaces.[139]

B. Preliminary assessment

147. Before collecting content from the Internet, open source investigators should conduct a preliminary assessment of any material that they identify in order to avoid over-collection and to comply with the principles of data minimization and focused investigation, as well as to ensure collecting the material does not violate the right to privacy of individuals. Open source investigators should consider the following factors to determine whether a digital item should be collected from the Internet.

---

[138] See OHCHR, "Freedom of expression vs incitement to hatred: OHCHR and the Rabat Plan of Action". Available at www.ohchr.org/EN/Issues/FreedomOpinion/Articles19-20/Pages/Index.aspx.

[139] See, e.g., Koenig and Egan, "Hiding in plain site: using online open source information to investigate sexual violence and gender-based crimes".

1. Relevance

148. Open source investigations should determine whether a digital item is prima facie relevant to a specific investigation. The relevance of any item depends on its content and source, as well as the objectives of an investigation and what is known about a situation. At the early stages of an investigation, it may be difficult to know what is relevant, which may result in investigators erring on the side of over-collection. Nevertheless, open source investigators should be able to articulate why they believe an item is potentially relevant and this assessment should be recorded (e.g. through a simple and user-friendly tagging or storage system that links the information collected to – for example – a place, date, incident, person or violation type that is being investigated).

2. Reliability

149. Open source investigators should determine whether the information or claims in digital content are prima facie reliable by reviewing and evaluating the content as well as the contextual information contained in the file. This could include checking embedded metadata, linked information and the source.[140] This process should involve trying to identify the original source of the material, which may require tracing the data's online provenance, uploader or author.

3. Removal

150. Open source investigators should assess whether a digital item is likely to be removed from the Internet or from public access. When content removal is likely, the most reliable known version of the content should be collected, even while further verification and investigation regarding earlier or better versions are conducted. The likelihood of content removal can be assessed based on a number of factors, including the presumed identity of the source, the location of the content and the compatibility of the content with the service provider's terms of service. For example,

graphic or offensive content, which could have high probative value for establishing crimes or violations, is some of the most likely content to be removed.

4. Safety

151. Open source investigators should determine whether a digital item is safe to collect or if additional precautions can and should be taken. Concerns are more likely to arise if collecting from a website that may contain corrupted items that could damage the internal system.

5. Subsequent duties

152. Open source investigators should determine what duties may arise if taking custody of a digital item, such as the duty to preserve it in a secure manner to comply with data protection laws.[141]

C. Collection

153. Collection is the act of gaining possession of online information through a screenshot, conversion to PDF, forensic download or other form of capture. Once digital content is identified and found to be relevant to an investigation and prima facie relevant and reliable for its purpose, an investigator must determine the proper method of collection. Collection methods may vary depending on whether the online content has potential evidentiary value in judicial processes, if it will be used or relied upon for decision-making purposes or if it will contribute to internal work product only. In cases simply involving work product, a screenshot or conversion to PDF may be sufficient, whereas content that has potential probative value may require a more thorough and sound method of capture (e.g. through assigning a hash value – see below).

154. Collection of online content can be performed manually, following a standard operating procedure, or can be automated, using a variety of tools or scripts. Regardless of the

---

[140] See chap. VI.E below on verification.

[141] See chap. VI.D below on preservation.

process, the information listed below should ideally be captured at the point of collection. This information may be useful to establish the authenticity of a digital item. This may be particularly important in the case of legal proceedings in which an item is offered as evidence, particularly if the author or creator is not identified, located or available to testify. Open source investigators should collect online content in its native format or in a state as close to its original format as possible. Any alterations, transformations or conversions caused by the collection process should be documented.

155. The following provides guidance on what to collect and how to collect it. There are several tools that assist with capturing the information below or it can be done manually. Whereas collecting all of the following information is considered a best practice, the first three items (uniform resource locator (URL), Hypertext Markup Language (HTML) source code and full-page capture) serve as a minimum standard for providing evidence in court. Of course, such standards will vary in different contexts, but capturing all the elements listed below will provide a strong foundation in any context:

(a) Target web address: the web address of the collected content, also known as the uniform resource locator (URL) or identifier (URI), should be recorded;

(b) Source code: investigators must capture the HTML source code of the web page, if applicable. HTML source code includes a lot more information than the visible portion of the website. The HTML source code will contribute to the authentication of the material collected;

(c) Full-page capture: investigators should first take a screen capture of the target web page with the date and time indicated. The reason for this process is to have the best possible representation of what was seen at the time of collection;

(d) Embedded media files: if downloading a web page with videos or images, for example, those specific items should also be extracted and collected from the web page;

(e) Embedded metadata: investigators should collect the additional metadata of the digital item, if available and applicable. Metadata can vary depending on the sources, but common metadata include uploader user identifier; post, picture or video identifier; upload date and time; geotag; hashtag; comments; and annotation;

(f) Contextual data: contextual content should also be collected if it is relevant to understanding the digital item. This may include comments on a video, image or post; upload information; and/or uploader/user information, such as a username, real name or biography. Whether surrounding information should be collected needs to be determined based on the specifics of the case and the digital item;

(g) Collection data: open source investigators must record all relevant data pertaining to the collection, such as the name of the collector, the IP address of the machine used to collect the information, the virtual identity used, if any, and a time stamp. Investigators should make sure that the system clock is accurate, preferably by synchronizing it with a Network Time Protocol server. The reason for this step is to ensure time-related metadata are accurately represented in the files collected. If a virtual identity is used to access the information collected, that should be noted;

(h) Hash value: hash values are a unique form of digital identification that confirm, through the use of cryptography, that the content collected is unique and has not been modified since the time of collection. At the point of collection, open source investigators should manually add – or the collection tool should automatically add – a hash value. There are many different types of hashes to choose from and the standards have evolved over time. Investigators should evaluate which hash to use based on the currently accepted standard.[142]

---

[142] The United States National Institute of Standards and Technology is one organization to look to for guidance on the current standard. See www.nist.gov.

156. In cases of automated collection, some of the processes described can be executed by tools designed to collect the relevant content and metadata. For each item collected, a technical report should be produced that includes the above information for the purpose of establishing the item's authenticity later on. Contextual information and all types of metadata should always be stored and preserved with the digital item, as explained in the following section.

D. Preservation

157. The permanence and availability of online information is often precarious. Social media platforms may remove content from their platforms in accordance with their terms of use, or users might choose to remove or edit their own uploaded content. Furthermore, online information can be easily decontextualized, lost, erased or corrupted.[143] If digital material is to remain accessible and usable for the purposes of ensuring legal accountability, it needs to be preserved for both the short and long term.[144] Generally, the purpose of digital preservation is to maintain accessibility.[145] When engaging in digital preservation for the purposes of ensuring legal accountability, however, the goal is to manage and maintain digital materials in a manner that helps ensure their accessibility, authenticity and potential use by accountability mechanisms, including their admissibility in legal proceedings.

Thus, digital preservation in the investigative context involves maintaining information over time so that the item collected remains independently understandable to its intended users with sufficient confirmation of its authenticity.

158. For long-term preservation, storage hardware and formats may require updating to ensure that materials remain accessible using contemporary devices.

1. Properties of a digital item that must be protected and preserved over time

159. According to archivists, the properties of a digital item that must be protected and preserved over time include its authenticity, availability, identity, persistence, renderability and understandability, as briefly described below.

(a) Authenticity

160. Authenticity refers to the ability to demonstrate that a digital item remains unchanged from when it was collected. It requires that a digital item remain unaltered while in an archive or that any modifications to it are documented.[146]

(b) Availability

161. Availability refers to the availability of a digital item in the simple sense of continually existing and being retrievable, as well as in the legal sense of securing the appropriate intellectual property rights to access and use the item.[147]

---

[143] Ng, "How to preserve open source information effectively".

[144] Ibid. p. 143. See United Nations Educational, Scientific and Cultural Organization, "Concept of digital preservation". Available at www.unesco.org/new/en/communication-and-information/access-to-knowledge/preservation-of-documentary-heritage/digital-heritage/concept-of-digital-preservation.

[145] Ng, "How to preserve open source information effectively".

[146] Ibid. Note that the use of the term "authenticity" in this context is different to its use in a legal context.

[147] Ibid.

(c)   Identity

162. Identity refers to a digital item's ability to be referenced. The digital item must be identifiable and distinguishable from other digital items, for example by being logged with an identifier, such as a unique identification number.[148]

(d)   Persistence

163. Persistence refers to the integrity and viability of a digital item in technical terms. The digital item's bit sequences must be intact, processible and retrievable.[149]

(e)   Renderability

164. Renderability refers to the ability of humans or machines to use or interact with a digital item using appropriate hardware and software.[150]

(f)   Understandability

165. Understandability refers to the ability of the intended users to interpret and understand a digital item.[151]

2.   Investigation-specific issues

166. Investigators should also consider and plan for investigation-specific issues that may or will arise during the preservation process.

(a)   Chain of custody

167. Chain of custody refers to the chronological documentation of the sequence of custodians of a piece of information or evidence, and documentation of the control, date and time, transfer, analysis and disposition of any such evidence. Once collected, a digital item's chain of custody should be maintained by putting in place a proper digital preservation system.

(b)   Evidentiary copy

168. An evidentiary copy is the digital item collected by an investigator in its original form that should not be altered or changed. Digital items should be stored in their original form. This means preserving a clean original of the collected digital item in all formats in which it was collected.

(c)   Working copies

169. A copy or copies of the digital item should be created for the purposes of analysis and stored separately so that investigators can work with the copy, rather than the original. This allows for minimal handling of the original and less risk of its being compromised or altered. Any and all changes to the item, including the making of copies, should be documented. If possible, separate storage systems should be used for evidentiary copies and working copies.

(d)   Storage

170. Storage helps ensure the persistence of digital items and the ability to find and retrieve them. Storage should not be thought of in passive terms, but as an active process involving ongoing, managed tasks and responsibilities. It includes permanent storage, in which storage media play a role, but also storage hierarchy management, media replacement, error checking, fixity checking (checking to ensure that the item has not been altered), disaster recovery, and locating and returning stored objects.[152] Digital information may be stored onsite (online or offline) or offsite (online or offline).[153] Storage options for digital content include a local hard drive or local removable media carrier; or a networked drive that is part of a local area network or a remote server or cloud storage system. Considerations related to storage choice

---

[148] Ibid.

[149] Ibid.

[150] Ibid.

[151] Ibid.

[152] Ibid., p. 154.

[153] Shira Scheindlin and Daniel J. Capra, *Electronic Discovery and Digital Evidence in a Nutshell* (Saint Paul, West Academic Publishing, 2009), pp. 21–22.

include storage capacity (space); access and control; backups; relevant law; and information security and data protection. Storage choices should also take speed, availability, cost, sustainability, storage management and retrieval systems into consideration.[154]

(i) Backup

171. If data loss or errors occur, an archivist or technician can attempt to recover the data. Ideally, the data will have been previously backed up or duplicated in a separate location. Information technology experts recommend having at least three copies of data, on at least two different types of storage, with at least one copy geographically separated from the other copies.

(ii) Degradation

172. One challenge of storage is that media degrade over time. Archivists can mitigate the risk of storage failure by using especially durable types of media; however, any storage device will eventually have or develop a defect, wear out or randomly fail. Even without total failure, data errors or file corruption can occur as stored media decay. It is therefore important to maintain backup copies and regularly monitor storage infrastructure and the permanence of stored files, such as by checking the hash values of random samples on a regular basis to ensure that no degradation has occurred.

(iii) Obsolescence

173. Digital files become obsolete when the hardware needed to access the data is no longer reasonably available or can no longer be reasonably maintained. Regardless of how durable any storage medium may be, it is also at risk of becoming obsolete, making it difficult or impossible to retrieve stored data. Therefore, investigations should ensure that they maintain and, when necessary, update storage media in order to maintain the renderability and availability of data.

(iv) Recovery

174. Digital files may be accidentally or purposefully deleted. When a user "deletes" a file on a computer, the deleted file's content will remain on the storage media until it is overwritten by another file.[155] Therefore, the more activity on the computer or other storage medium, the faster it will be overwritten and become unrecoverable. Most computers have software utilities built into the operating system to allow for the recovery of deleted files. In addition, data recovery software can be purchased and sometimes used to "undelete" files. Open source investigators may need to enlist the help of information technology specialists to access deleted data.

(v) Refreshing

175. Refreshing involves copying content from one storage medium to another. It targets only media obsolescence and is not a comprehensive preservation strategy. Refreshing, however, should be seen as an integral part of a greater retention strategy.[156]

E. Verification

176. Verification refers to the process of establishing the accuracy or validity of information that has been collected online. Verification of open source information can be done as part of an all-source analysis – including information from closed and confidential sources – or based exclusively on open sources. Verification is broken down into three separate considerations: the source, the digital item or file, and the content, which should be looked at collectively and compared for consistency.

1. Source analysis

177. Source analysis is the process of assessing a source's credibility and reliability. The online environment presents challenges to source analysis as many sources are anonymous or pseudonymous. In order to

---

[154] Ng, "How to preserve open source information effectively", p. 156.

[155] Scheindlin and Capra, *Electronic Discovery and Digital Evidence in a Nutshell*, p. 24.

[156] Cornell University Library, "Digital imaging tutorial". Available at http://preservationtutorial.library.cornell.edu/tutorial/preservation/preservation-03.html.

properly analyse sources of information, open source investigators must first identify the correct source or sources to analyse, which means attributing the information to its original source. Attribution analysis refers to determining the source of the digital information, which might be a specific website, subscriber or user of a given account or platform, or the identity of the persons who authored, created or uploaded certain content. Attribution analysis is not always possible and may require additional online and real-world investigative steps or advanced search and analysis techniques. While identifying authorship is helpful, a lack of it is not generally critical for establishing an online item's authenticity, as there are other ways to authenticate open source information.

(a) Provenance

178. Provenance relates to the origin or earliest known existence of something. When it comes to online content, provenance can refer to the earliest appearance online or the original item before it was uploaded to the Internet. In the case of online content, it is preferable to refer to the "first copy found online" rather than "the first copy online" since the original may have been removed. Even when investigators are confident that they have found the first version of, for example, a video or other information from online open sources, they cannot be certain of its provenance because of the existence of closed channels, such as emails and private messaging groups, which may have been used to share the item before its public appearance online.[157]

(b) Credibility

179. A source's posting history, online activity and Internet presence may contain relevant information that weighs against or in favour of a source's credibility. Open source investigators should examine a source's online presence and posting history, which may even help catch a deliberate attempt to deceive. For example, if posting about events in a particular country,

does a source's surrounding posts suggest that he or she is actually in that country?

(c) Independence and impartiality

180. Investigations should examine a source's impartiality. This can be done by looking at any groups, organizations or affiliations with which individuals are associated, as well as how they make money and from whom they receive funding. Are there connections to or relationships with any of the parties involved in the case or incident being investigated? In considering the independence of sources, examine whether they may be associated with relevant entities (e.g. parties to a conflict). The ideology of a source and any group affiliation may also be relevant. For all sources, investigators should examine and uncover their underlying motivations, interests or agendas, and the degree to which these might influence their veracity.

(d) Specificity

181. The more precise the information and claims, the easier they will be to prove or disprove. Broad and vague claims tend to be more difficult to critically assess.

(e) Attenuation

182. Texts drafted contemporaneously with the events that they reference tend to be viewed as more reliable than those produced long after the events have occurred.[158] This factor may be challenging for open source investigators when it is unclear when a digital text was created.

2. Technical analysis

183. Technical analysis refers to the analysis of a digital item itself, whether it is a document, image or video. In order to test the integrity of a file, that is whether it has been digitally altered, manipulated or modified, open source investigators may find it appropriate to subject it to digital forensic examination, sometimes referred to as digital investigative analysis. The following are components of such an analysis.

---

[157] E.g., one user may email a photograph to another user, who then uploads it to social media. Thus, the photograph originated with the emailer not the poster.

[158] Institute for International Criminal Investigations, *Investigators Manual*, 5th ed. (The Hague, 2012), p. 88.

(a) Metadata

184. Metadata are data that describe and give information about other data. They can be created by the user that generated an item, other users, a communication service provider or any device upon which data are created, transferred, received or viewed. Metadata are relevant in describing an item and the circumstances of its generation, dissemination or alteration. Metadata might include the creator of a file, its date of creation, upload data, modifications, file size and geodata. Metadata can be embedded in a file, visible on a web page or present in source code. Some metadata may be stripped before or during uploading, or as a result of using social media applications, but if they are available, they should be reviewed in case they can help establish authenticity. Original metadata may be lost because platforms often transcode uploaded media to optimize them for online viewing, sharing or playback. In such cases, the metadata will be a reflection of the new file, not the original. Where metadata have been stripped, open source researchers should seek other ways to verify an item.

(b) Exchangeable image file format data

185. Exchangeable image file format is a type of metadata that specifies the formats for images, sound and ancillary tags used by digital cameras, scanners and other systems handling image and sound files recorded by digital cameras.

(c) Source code

186. The source code is the programming behind any web page or software. In the case of websites, this code can be viewed by anyone using various tools, even a web browser itself. A website's source code is easy to view using a number of freely available tools. It may contain meta-content or hidden or manipulated content and will show the link structure and broken links.

3. Content analysis

187. Content analysis is the process by which the information contained within a video, image, document or statement is assessed for its authenticity and veracity. Content analysis is similarly multifaceted and involves analysing visual clues or, for example, corroborating the image with the metadata. The characteristics of the online environment give rise to numerous issues that can affect the actual or perceived validity or veracity of information from online open sources. These include circular reporting, decontextualization of information and misinterpretation. Content data are data contained in the digital item, such as a video, image, audio recording, document or unstructured text.

(a) Unique identifiers

188. When tasked with verifying visual content, investigators should begin by looking for unique or identifying features. Such features might include buildings, flora and fauna, people, symbols and insignia. Special caution should be used when analysing human features with the goal of identifying a specific person.[159] Identification practices usually require specific skills, such as those acquired over time and through the specialized training of a forensic expert. Lay analyses can be inaccurate, prejudicial and/or otherwise problematic if conducted by untrained professionals.

(b) Objectively verifiable information

189. Often, it can be helpful to start by identifying what might qualify as "objectively verifiable information". For example, the weather on a specific day, the name and rank of a commanding officer or the location of a building could all be objectively verifiable.

---

[159] Forensic analysis and identification of human features with tools or human analysis (e.g. facial recognition, gait analysis etc.) require a forensic expert. See Nina M. van Mastrigt and others, "Critical review of the use and scientific basis of forensic gait analysis", *Forensic Sciences Research*, vol. 3, No. 3 (2018), pp. 183–193 (available at www.tandfonline.com/doi/full/10.1080/20961790.2018.1 503579); Royal Society and Royal Society of Edinburgh, "Forensic gait analysis: a primer for courts" (London, 2017) (available at: https://royalsociety.org/-/media/about-us/programmes/science-and-law/royal-society-forensic-gait-analysis-primer-for-courts.pdf). See also European Network of Forensic Science, *Best Practice Manual for Facial Image Comparison* (2018) (available at http://enfsi.eu/wp-content/uploads/2017/06/ENFSI-BPM-DI-01.pdf); National Center for Audio and Video Forensics, "Height analysis of surveillance video" (available at https://ncavf.com/what-we-do/forensic-height-analysis).

An assessment of open source material should include an examination of its content against such objectively verifiable information.

(c) Geolocation

190. Geolocation is the identification or estimation of the location of an object, an activity or the location from which an item was generated. For example, it may be possible to determine the location from which a video or photograph downloaded from the Internet was taken using geolocation techniques. Such techniques could include, for example, identifying unique geographic features in a photograph with their actual location on a map.

(d) Chronolocation

191. Chronolocation is the corroboration of the dates and times of the events depicted in a piece of information, usually visual imagery. For example, it may be possible to determine the time of day a photograph was taken by examining the length of the shadows made by sunlight, along with other indicators.

(e) Completeness

192. An incomplete document or video clip may still be probative, however, the gap(s) may have an impact on the weight that can be attributed to an item. Therefore, when collecting open source information, it is important to capture a target file in its entirety and, when relevant, to capture the surrounding context.

(f) Internal consistency

193. An assessment of internal consistency may be made in relation to a single piece of information from an online open source or in relation to a body of information from a particular source (and/or sources with the same provenance or authorship). An assessment of the internal consistency of a single piece of online information seeks to establish whether the information is consistent and coherent on its own terms. An internally consistent piece or body of information should not contradict itself.

(g) External corroboration

194. External corroboration is provided by information that lies outside a digital item itself but that coincides with and thus supports the veracity of the item's content.

F. Investigative analysis

195. Investigative analysis is the practice of reviewing and interpreting factual information to develop substantive findings relevant to decision-making or case-building. The volume and varying quality of open source information necessitates a well-structured approach to analysis.

196. Before undergoing certain types of analysis, open source information may first need to be processed. Processing may involve translation of foreign languages or aggregation of different data sets to assist in analysing the behaviour of individuals, locations and objects, as well as relationships or networks, movements, activities or transactions. It can also involve changing the nature or format of a digital item to make it compatible with specific software. Common types of data-processing include:

(a) Translation: if the data are in a language that is not spoken by the investigators or not processed by the software necessary to review the material, the data may need to be translated before further steps are taken;

(b) Aggregation: investigators may need to aggregate different data sets into one larger data set in order to analyse it;

(c) Reformatting: to make the data more easily searchable or retrievable, investigators may need to change the format of a digital item.

197. It is advisable to only process working copies of a digital item, as opposed to the original or evidentiary copy. Any processing of a digital item should be documented. If investigators use digital technologies to process data, for example, analysing data using algorithms, including natural language processing and deep learning, they must be aware of the risk of bias in processing such data.

198. Once processed, information can then be analysed. Analytical work products of open source information will vary depending on purpose, type and scope of the underlying source information, the production timeline

and its audience. These will be developed according to the needs of an investigation and could include charts, summaries, glossaries, dictionaries and visual aids, including maps and mapping exercises.[160]

199. Investigators should apply rigorous standards to ensure the objectivity, timeliness, relevance and accuracy of the data and conclusions contained in analytical products, and to protect privacy and other human rights considerations, especially when dealing with personally identifiable information. Such information should only be included in products for which investigators have obtained the consent of the persons involved and it serves a direct investigative purpose. It should also be considered in light of the legal and ethical limitations surrounding its use.[161]

200. The following sections contain common types of analysis that may be used to further investigative objectives using open source information.

1. Image/video comparison analysis

201. Comparison analysis or comparison science is the process of comparing features of objects, persons and/or locations to other unknown and/or known items when at least one of the items in question is an image. It is the analysis of the content of images and videos, including elements of comparison between different items and features, and their image quality and visual settings (light, perspective etc.). While many lay people now know the basics of image comparison analysis, the assistance of an expert who is qualified and certified in forensic video analysis and/or digital forensics may help in providing scientific analysis, including an expert opinion. Human rights and other types of investigations may also benefit from such expertise to give further weight to their findings.

2. Image/video interpretation analysis

202. Related to image/video comparison is image/video interpretation analysis, which involves analysing a digital item to understand its visual content. For example, analysis of gunshots, wounds, blood, vehicles, weapons and military assets or analysis of the speed of a moving vehicle or the age of an individual are all part of image/video interpretation analysis. It can be done by analysts for investigative purposes or by forensic or subject matter experts in the case of establishing facts in legal proceedings or human rights findings.

3. Spatial analysis

203. Spatial analysis or geospatial analysis may include visual content analysis and metadata analysis for items that offer geographic coordinates or place names. Spatial analysis involves examining different objects and landscape features, at an appropriate resolution, and checking against satellite or other images, geodata and maps, proper case and context knowledge, and Geographic Information System[162] tools.

4. Actor mapping

204. Actor mapping is a technique for understanding key actors and identifying power relationships and channels of influence.[163] Thus, it begins with identifying the key actors and then mapping out the relationships among them.

5. Social network analysis

205. Similar to actor mapping, social network analysis is the mapping and measuring of relationships between people, groups, organizations, computers, URLs and other connected information/knowledge entities.[164]

---

160 See chap. VII below on reporting on findings.

161 See chap. III above on the legal framework.

162 The Geographic Information System is a computerized database for managing and analyzing spatial data.

163 OHCHR, *Manual on Human Rights Monitoring*, chap. 8 on analysis, p. 24.

164 Orgnet, "Social network analysis: an introduction". Available at www.orgnet.com/sna.html.

People and groups are often referred to as nodes, while links show relationships between the nodes. Social network analysis uses the connections on social media and other mobile or web-based platforms to establish and understand relationships among individuals. Analysing connection or link data can be done manually by an investigator or using analytics software.

6. Incident mapping

206. Incident mapping is an analytical technique used to establish the temporal and geographic relationships among different incidents, which in the context of international criminal and human rights violations may refer to the location of such violations or crimes, including

prior and subsequent events. It may also include mapping other relevant events, such as where and when statements were made by alleged perpetrators.

7. Crime/violation pattern analysis

207. In the context of national law enforcement, a crime pattern is a group of two or more crimes reported to or discovered by law enforcement that are unique because they share at least one commonality in the type of crime; behaviour of the offenders or victims; characteristics of the offender(s), victims or targets; property taken; or the locations of occurrence.[165] Similarly, crime and violation patterns can be established in international criminal and human rights cases based on open source information.

---

[165] International Association of Crime Analysts, "Crime pattern definitions for tactical analysis", Standards, Methods and Technology Committee White Paper 2011-01, p. 1.

REPORTING ON FINDINGS

CHAPTER SUMMARY

- The findings of an open source investigation, referring to either the data collected or the conclusions drawn from that data, can be reported orally, visually or in writing.

- Investigators should consider which formats are most appropriate to their mandates and intended audiences – taking into account factors such as the technological literacy of the audiences and accessibility, objectivity, transparency and security – when deciding on (a) the formats to use and (b) the data to include.

208. This chapter describes the ways in which open source investigations – including the methodologies, raw data and analytical findings – can be presented or reported on. In many cases, open source information will be presented in tandem with other information gathered through other methods of investigation. Presentations can take many forms, including written reports, oral reports or visual reports, or any combination of those forms. Reports may be for internal use or external publication and may be considered as expert or non-expert depending on a number of factors. Reports should ensure the following elements:

(a) Accuracy: reports should accurately represent the data collected.[166] Exculpatory information should be included, as should an explanation of any redactions or gaps;

(b) Attribution: reports should clearly distinguish between content that is in the public domain or general unclassified information, information that is classified or otherwise restricted and content that reflects the judgment or opinion of investigators and/or other professionals. Investigators or others reporting on open source information should also conduct due diligence and gain proper permissions for the use of content that might belong to others, for example by securing any necessary intellectual property rights;

(c) Completeness: findings should provide an indication of the completeness of the underlying data, especially if data are deliberately excluded;

(d) Confidentiality: despite being found in open source settings, reports should consider which material should be left out or redacted to protect confidentiality or otherwise minimize risks, in particular the potential risks for sources, witnesses, victims and members of communities linked with the open source information;

(e) Language: reports should use neutral language and avoid emotive or emotional language. They should state facts clearly without overusing adjectives or emphasis. Reports need to be written in gender-sensitive language. Ideally, public reports should be made available in the languages of the affected communities in addition to any official languages used by the investigators or investigating bodies;

(f) Transparency: reports should state clearly how the investigators went about their work, and their aims, processes and methods. Normally, this will be included in a report's methodology section but it should also guide descriptions throughout the text. The descriptions should be as transparent as possible without creating security vulnerabilities, for example by revealing confidential information.

A. Written reporting

209. An open source investigation may be presented in writing, which may include internal reports and reports to clients, as well as public reports. One method of communicating analytical findings is through a written report, which may include reports by NGOs, commissions of inquiry, fact-finding missions and the United Nations, and expert reports for a court or tribunal, among others.[167] Digital open source information will often be integrated with other forms of open and closed source data and analysis. Written reports should analyse the information collected in order to draw logical conclusions, estimates and predictions. Reports should reflect sound methodology and be able to explain that methodology to the target audience. The veracity and integrity of the underlying information in a report is crucial. Bad data will lead to bad conclusions.[168]

---

[166] See chap. II.B above on methodological principles.

[167] For an example of a written digital open source investigation report, see, e.g., Human Rights Investigations Lab, "Chemical strikes on Al-Lataminah: March 25 & 30, 2017 – a student-led open source investigation" (Berkeley, Human Rights Center, University of California, Berkeley, School of Law, 2018).

[168] Based on the circumstances and confidentiality requirements, peer review is recommended to ensure the accuracy and quality of data, as well as the analysis and findings drawn from that data.

210. Written reports should include the following sections unless there is a justifiable and articulated reason not to, for example, the need to keep some online investigative techniques, methods and sources confidential:

    (a) Investigative objectives: reports should include the investigative objectives, and underlying mandates or client instructions, including well-defined, articulable research questions;

    (b) Methodology: reports should include the research methods to enable replicability and to allow audiences to understand and assess the credibility of the information and findings of the investigations, including what is covered;

    (c) Performed activities: reports should include a summary of the activities performed that are material to the findings or the assessment of the quality of analysis, including the activities to identify the underlying data, what was collected and what was analysed;

    (d) Underlying data and sources: reports should include a description of the underlying data, including the sources and quality thereof;

    (e) Gaps or uncertainties: reports should identify any gaps or uncertainties in the underlying data or the analysis that might be material to the findings;

    (f) Results and recommendations: reports should include the investigators' interpretations of the data or findings based on the analyses of the data, noting caveats and new leads.

B. Oral reporting

211. If the findings of an open source investigation reach a courtroom, investigators might have to testify as witnesses; thus, presenting their investigations through oral testimony. Other forms of oral reporting can include presentations before truth commissions, NGO forums, people's tribunals or media events.

212. Anyone required to orally present the findings of their open source investigation must be able to clearly and accurately explain the work, including the methodology applied and tools used. This will ensure that the oral testimony and the findings described are treated with due weight.

213. In the case of legal proceedings, it is often the heads of investigations who will have to testify, and they should be able to speak about the work of their teams. That requires, of course, that they know what their teams have done and can answer questions about the roles performed and the reasoning underlying any decision-making concerning the scope of an investigation, its methods, the tools used etc. Investigators may be either expert witnesses or lay witnesses. Expert witnesses – witnesses considered experts because of their experience, knowledge, skill, training, education or related credentials – can testify about the conclusions they reached and other analytical work product. Lay witnesses are generally limited to testifying about facts and, specifically, those that they have personally observed.

C. Visual reporting

214. Data visualization is the graphical representation of information in the form of, for example, charts, graphs, tables, maps and infographics, which provide an accessible way to see and understand trends, outliers and patterns in data.[169] It can include charts and other graphical representations of data in space and time; graphs (including those that demonstrate mathematical connections, trends or relationships); network graphs, which demonstrate relationships among various persons; and statistical charts and diagrams. Two-dimensional and three-dimensional maps for visualizing objects in space

---

[169] Examples of visual reporting in different contexts include the digital platforms used as demonstrative evidence in *Prosecutor v. Ahmad Al Faqi Al Mahdi* at the International Criminal Court and *Prosecutor v. Salim Jamil Ayyash et al.* at the Special Tribunal for Lebanon; report of the detailed findings of the independent international commission of inquiry on the protests in the Occupied Palestinian Territory (available at www.ohchr.org/EN/HRBodies/HRC/RegularSessions/Session40/Documents/A_HRC_40_74_CRP2.pdf); BBC Africa Eye, "Cameroon atrocity: what happened after Africa Eye found who killed this woman", BBC News, 30 May 2019 (available at www.bbc.com/news/av/world-africa-48432122/cameroon-atrocity-what-happened-after-africa-eye-found-who-killed-this-woman). See also, generally, the work of Forensic Architecture and SITU Research.

and time, and three-dimensional reconstructions of various sites, including crime scenes, also form part of the data visualization repertoire.[170] These tools can be helpful to understand large quantities of data, which is often the case in open source investigations, or to better understand complex factual scenarios.

215. Other types of data visualizations include:

(a) Mind maps: a mind map is a graphical means of representing ideas and concepts and how they relate to each other. Mind maps structure information in a way that makes that information easier to analyse, synthesize and comprehend. Mind maps will often include an explanation of how the underlying data were discovered;

(b) Flowcharts: a flowchart is a graphical representation of a sequence of events, such as the steps embedded in an algorithm, workflow or similar processes;

(c) Infographics: an infographic is an illustrated representation of an idea or concept; it can be used to represent statistical information.

216. Open source information can be presented in a variety of ways, ranging from an audiovisual display of a single video or website to interactive, digital and aggregated multimedia presentations.[171] Visual demonstrations and illustrations, or digital platforms, may be used to display information in a way that makes it easier for the intended audiences to understand the underlying facts. Examples include timelines, composite photographs (such as a 360-degree view of a crime scene) and edited videos.

217. In the case of presenting data-visualization and multimedia evidence in a courtroom, or to other public audiences, investigators should understand which technical issues might arise, including which platforms lawyers may need to make their presentations as helpful as possible to fact finders. A range of factors should be taken into account in deciding the best form for representing the underlying data. Such factors include the intended audiences and their comfort levels with potential formats and their ability to understand the information being communicated.[172] Ultimately, all presentations should further the goal of illuminating the facts relevant to a case in a manner that is probative and not prejudicial and should comply with the legal and ethical requirements of the jurisdiction in which the information is presented.

---

[170] See, e.g., International Criminal Court Digital Platform: Timbuktu, Mali (developed by SITU Research as an asset for the *Al Mahdi* case at the International Criminal Court). Available at http://icc-mali.situplatform.com. See also a variety of online open source investigations and their visual reports at Forensic Architecture. Available at https://forensic-architecture.org/methodology/osint.

[171] While not provided for a court, the New York Times Visual Investigations Team has produced a number of visual explainers designed to aggregate online open source information, support analysis of complex incidents and report on those findings. See, e.g., Nicholas Casey, Christoph Koettl and Deborah Acosta, "Footage contradicts U.S. claim that Nicolás Maduro burned aid convoy", *New York Times*, 10 March 2019 (available at www.nytimes.com/2019/03/10/world/americas/venezuela-aid-fire-video.html); Malachy Browne and others, "10 minutes. 12 gunfire bursts. 30 videos. Mapping the Las Vegas massacre", *New York Times*, 21 October 2017 (available at www.nytimes.com/video/us/100000005473328/las-vegas-shooting-timeline-12-bursts.html).

[172] See Alexa Koenig, "Open source evidence and human rights cases: a modern social history", in *Digital Witness: Using Open Source Information for Human Rights Investigation, Documentation and Accountability*, Sam Dubberley, Alexa Koenig and Daragh Murray, eds. (Oxford, Oxford University Press, 2020), pp. 38–40.

GLOSSARY

SUMMARY

■ Terms and definitions used in open source investigations or those that may arise in relevant or related resources.

218. This chapter contains terms and definitions that may be helpful to open source investigators. Not all terms are used in the Protocol but are included because they may arise in relevant or related resources.

Air gap: when a digital device is not directly connected to the Internet or any network, therefore providing security for the information held by that device.

Algorithm: a well-defined procedure or set of instructions that allows a computer to solve a problem or respond to a predetermined scenario.

Anonymization: the process of making it impossible to identify a specific individual.

Application programming interface (API): code that allows software computer programs to communicate with each other.

Artificial intelligence (AI): a branch of computer science dedicated to developing programming for machines to learn how to react to unknown variables and adapt to new environments.

Beacon: a mechanism for tracking user activity and behaviour. Beacons are made from a small and unobtrusive (often invisible) element in a web page (as small as a single, transparent pixel) that, when rendered by the browser, communicates details about the browser and computer being used to a third party.

Big data: large data sets that can be analysed to detect correlations between data points and reveal patterns that may help with predictive abilities. The key characteristics of big data are volume and complexity.

Blockchain: a cryptography-based technology whereby an open, distributed ledger comprised of "blocks" can be used to record transactions between two parties or entities efficiently and in a verifiable and permanent way.

Boolean search: an Internet search technique that allows users to combine keywords with operators or modifiers (i.e., AND, NOT, OR) to narrow search results and thereby provide more relevant and specific search results.

Captcha: acronym for completely automated public Turing test to tell computers and humans apart is a type of challenge–response test used in computing to determine whether a user is human.

Chat room: a website on the Internet that allows users to have real-time conversations online.

Cloud computing: an operations model that enables storage, processing and analysis of data over an intranet or the Internet. There are three types of cloud: private, public and hybrid.

Cookie: a small piece of data that is sent by a website and stored either in a user's computer memory or written to a computer's disk for use by a browser. Cookies are often necessary for a website to function efficiently – offering the ability for a user's website preferences and identity details to be stored, removing the need for constant data entry by users during their subsequent visits.

Cryptographic signature: a mathematical process for verifying the authenticity of a digital item. Using an algorithm, one can generate two keys that are mathematically linked: one private and one public. To create a digital signature, software is used to create a hash of the electronic data. The private key is then used to encrypt the hash.

Cryptography: the practice of digitally encoding or decoding information.

Dark web: that part of the Internet that is only accessible by means of special software, allowing users and website operators to remain anonymous and untraceable.

Data mining: the practice of examining and extracting data from databases in order to generate knowledge or new information.

Digital archive: a collection of documents, web pages or electronic records. The term may also refer to a formal or informal organization that accepts responsibility for preserving information and making it available to authorized users.

Digital preservation: the policies and strategies required to manage and maintain digital information with enduring value over time, so that the digital information is accessible and usable by its intended users in the future.

Domain name: a label that identifies a network domain. Within the Internet, domain names are formed by the rules and procedures of the Domain Name System (DNS). In general, a domain name represents an Internet Protocol (IP) resource, such as a personal computer used to access the Internet, a server hosting a website, the website itself, or any other service communicated via the Internet.

Domain name registrant: the person, company or other entity who owns or holds a domain name.

Domain name system (DNS): the system through which the assignment of domain names is regulated.

Dragnet: in the online context, a broad automated collection or surveillance system.

Embedded data: data stored in a source file or web page.

Encryption: the process of making data inaccessible without a decryption key.

Hash or hash value: calculations that can be run on any type of digital file to generate a fixed-length alphanumeric string that can be used as evidence that a digital file has not been modified. This string will remain the same every time the calculation is run as long as the file does not change.

Hypertext Markup Language (HTML): a programming language that is used to design web pages accessed through a browser.

Hypertext Transfer Protocol (HTTP): a protocol underlying the Internet that defines how data are transferred and received.

Internet Assigned Numbers Authority (IANA): an organization that oversees the global allocation of IP addresses, autonomous system numbers and domain name systems.

Internet Corporation for Assigned Names and Numbers (ICANN): an organization responsible for ensuring the Internet's stable and secure operation by coordinating the maintenance and procedures of several databases related to the name and numerical spaces of the Internet.

Internet forum (also known as a discussion board): a website through which users can post messages and have conversations. Forums usually contain longer messages than those seen in chat rooms and are more likely to archive content.

Internet Protocol (IP) address: any digital device that connects to the Internet has an IP address. There are two types of IP addresses: IPv4 (32-bit number) and IPv6 (128-bit number). An IP address can be used to identify computers and other devices on the Internet.

Internet service provider (ISP): an entity that provides Internet users with services to access and use the Internet.

Intranet: a private computer network that uses Internet protocols and network connectivity to establish an in-house version of the Internet.

Local area network (LAN): a collection of digital devices connected to the same network in a defined physical location.

Machine learning: a type of artificial intelligence that uses statistical techniques to give computers the ability to "learn" from data, without being explicitly programmed.

Malware: malicious software that is designed to cause harm to a digital device, network, server or user. There are many different types of malware, including viruses, Trojan horses, ransomware, adware and spyware.

Metadata: are data about data. They contain information about an electronic file that is either embedded in or associated with the file. Metadata often include a file's characteristics and history, such as its name, size, and dates of creation and modification. Metadata may describe how, when, and by whom a digital file was collected, created, accessed, modified and formatted.

Native file: a file in its original format.

Portable Document Format (PDF): a fixed-layout file format that preserves the format of a document (including fonts, spacing and imagery) regardless of the software, hardware and operating systems used to open and view that document. Converting a file from its original format to a PDF strips its metadata, providing a static image of the document.

Predictive software: software that uses predictive algorithms and machine learning to analyse data to make predictions about the future or unknown events or behaviours.

Pseudonymization: the processing of personal data in such a manner that the information can no longer be attributed to a specific data subject without the use of additional information.

Scraping: a method of extracting mass quantities of data from websites.

Social engineering: the psychological manipulation of a person in order to gain unauthorized access to information. It is similar to hacking but involves exploiting a human vulnerability rather than a technical vulnerability. There are many different types of social engineering, including phishing and spear phishing.

Stripping: a technological process for removing metadata from a file without converting that file to other formats.

Structured data: data or information that conforms to a rigid format in a repository (typically a database but could also be a set of filled forms) so that its elements are readily available for processing and analysis.

Surface web: that portion of the Internet that can be accessed through any browser and searched using traditional search engines.

Tracker: a type of cookie that exploits the ability of a browser to keep a record of which web pages have been visited, which search criteria have been entered etc. Trackers are generally persistent cookies that keep a running log of the behaviour of a particular visitor.

Traffic data: any data processed for the purpose of conveying information on an electronic communications network or for the billing in respect of that communication. Such data includes data relating to the routing, time or duration of a communication.

Uniform resource locator (URL): the location of a web page on the Internet. It is the same as a web address.

Unstructured data: data and information that come in many different forms, that are not organized in a rigid format and thus are not easy to process and analyse. They are typically text but they can also include image, audio and video files.

Virtual machine: software that emulates a computer system.

Virtual private network (VPN): a secure network or system of secure nodes that use encryption and other security processes to ensure that only authorized users can access the network. VPNs mask the IP address and prevent data from being intercepted.

Web-based service provider: an entity that provides services and products on the Internet, such as a social media company.

Web crawler (also referred to as a web spider or spiderbot): a program that systematically browses the Internet according to an automated scrip to download and index the websites visited.

WHOIS: a record that identifies who owns a particular domain name based on the entity that registered it. Open source investigators may use a WHOIS lookup tool as part of the source analysis and verification process.

World Wide Web (WWW): an information space in which documents and other web resources are identified by URLs, which may be interlinked by hypertext and are accessible through the Internet. The resources of the World Wide Web may be accessed by users using a software application called a web browser

VIII. GLOSSARY

ANNEXES

Annex I

Online investigation plan template

Investigation reference number:

Date of assessment:

Investigation summary: *subject matter, and territorial and temporal scope of the investigation*

1. Objectives and planned activities

This includes the objectives of and strategy for the online investigation, as well as specific activities with a timeline for their implementation.

2. Summary of digital landscape assessment

This includes an assessment of the digital landscape in the geographic territory under investigation, such as the popular social media, mobile applications and other technologies, as well as who has access to and uses those technologies.

3. Risk mitigation strategy and protection measures

This includes the key findings of the digital threat and risk assessment, along with a strategy for identifying, managing and responding to such threats.

4. Mapping of relevant actors

This includes a list of first responders who may have collected potentially relevant online content that has since disappeared, digital archives and Internet and web-based service providers, which might have original versions or additional metadata for online content that can be acquired through a request for assistance. While non-legal investigators may not have the legal authority to request closed source information, contacts within Internet service providers may nevertheless be valuable in answering questions and assisting users in navigating their platforms.

5. Roles and responsibilities

This includes a determination of the roles and responsibilities of team members and should include identification of a focal point who will coordinate online activities. This may also include an assessment of who will potentially be responsible if called to testify in court.

6. Resources

This includes an assessment of staffing needs (numbers of investigators, diversity and inclusivity of staff members), as well as any specialized training and equipment needed for online investigative activities.

7. Documentation

This includes specific directions on how and where team members should document their online investigative activities.

Annex II

Digital threat and risk assessment template

Investigation reference number:

Date of assessment:

Investigation summary: *subject matter, and territorial and temporal scope of the investigation*

Investigative objectives:

1. What are your assets?

People (disaggregated by gender):

Tangible property:

Intangible property (e.g. data):

2. What are your vulnerabilities?

3. Which types of threats could exploit those vulnerabilities and harm your assets?

4. Who are the potential threat actors?

A. What are their interests?

B. What are their capabilities?

C. What is the probability of an attack?

5. Which risk-mitigating measures are possible/appropriate? Is there a need to respond to different risks faced by different genders?

The following should be considered:

• Physical harm

• Digital harm

• Psychosocial harm

Annex III

Digital landscape assessment template

Investigation reference number:

Date of assessment:

Investigation summary: *subject matter, and territorial and temporal scope of the investigation*

Investigative objectives:

An asterisk (*) indicates that investigators should take into consideration various factors such as age, gender, location and other relevant demographic information.

1. Relevant parties (i.e. specific communities, armed groups etc.). Indicate if there is any difference in technology use or online representation by gender, age or disability among each of the parties.

2. Relevant languages (including slang and other insider languages)*

3. Frequently used search engines*

4. Popular social media platforms*

5. Popular websites*

6. Internet usage/penetration (disaggregated by gender, age etc.)

7. Mobile telephone/operating system preferences (disaggregated by gender, age etc.)

8. Popular mobile applications (disaggregated by gender, age etc.)

9. Telecommunications providers

10. Connectivity: Wi-Fi/cell tower locations

11. Relevant laws (freedom of expression, access to information, privacy)

12. Media outlets and reporters (online presence)

13. Open databases (e.g. of government data, NGO/researcher data)

14. Paid databases (e.g. of government data, private company/researcher data)

15. Representativeness of online content (included versus excluded groups)

Annex IV

Online data collection form

1. Collector information

Investigation:

Collector:

Collector IP address:

Start of collection (date/time stamp):

End of collection (date/time stamp):

2. Target information

Web address (URL):

HTML source code:

Screenshot:

Captured data:

IP address(es):

3. Collection package information

Collection package file name:

Collection package hash list:

Hash of collection package hash list file:

4. Services used

Software product(s):

Time service:

IP service:

WHOIS service:

Annex V

Considerations for validating new tools

Features

Open-source versus closed-source code

Paid versus free

Owner's (individual's or company's) identity, affiliations or interests

Funding (how and how well is the tool funded? What is the product's likely lifespan?)

Security questions

Who owns the tool or the underlying code?

Is the underlying code open source or closed source?

Is the tool independently audited?

Where will any collected data be stored?

Who will have access to any collected data?

What is the tool's security infrastructure?

Which legal obligations may affect the security of using the tool?

If there is a breach of law, is there a right to remedy?

Operational questions

What is the tool's functionality?

What is the tool's usability?

What is the owner's, provider's or tool's user support capacity?

How frequently is the tool updated?

How compatible is the tool with other systems?